Don't Do Shots with Strangers

The All-Inclusive Guide to All-Inclusive Vacations

Rob Durham

Copyright © 2019 Rob Durham

All rights reserved.

No part of this book may be used or reproduced, stored in or introduced into a retrieval system, or transmitted in any form or by means without the express written consent of the publisher of this book.

Published and printed in the United States of America

ISBN: 9781706111047

For Beth,

My companion through life, my love

TABLE OF CONTENTS

	Acknowledgments	i
1	Picture It	1
2	Choosing the Best Resort for Your Money	3
3	Preparing for Your Trip	17
4	Welcome to the Good Life	29
5	Avoiding Rookie Mistakes	38
6	Making the Most of Vacation	43
7	Services and Meals	59
8	Staying Active	69
9	Day Trips	81
10	Heading Home	99
	Appendix of Resorts, Checklists, and Resources	104
	About the Author	108

ACKNOWLEDGMENTS

Thank you to Lelah Thomas for the VIP treatment on our travels.
Thank you to my editor, Kari Vo.
Thank you Caleb Dunn and Jeff Hawk for going above and beyond with feedback as beta readers.
Thank you to Roberta, our favorite mezcal expert in Mexico.

"The ocean breathes salty, won't you carry it in?
In your head, in your mouth, in your soul."

—Isaac Brock, Modest Mouse

Chapter 1
Picture It

White sand, turquoise water, heavenly sunsets...all in someone else's pictures. That's when the envy hits hardest, right? You're scrolling through social media minutes before another taxing day at your job while everyone else is taking an amazing trip. When will it be your turn? Yes, there was that trip a few years ago to some lake where the water was too cold for swimming and instead of sand, you got rocks and cigarette butts, but you need somewhere better. No more indoor water parks overrun by children. No more dining at seafood restaurants where the servers dress like pirates. No more hauling coolers of canned beer to overcrowded beaches.

It's your turn for the ultimate getaway. You deserve a trip you'll remember the rest of your life. A vacation that actually *feels* like one. It's time to make everyone else envious, so start planning an all-inclusive vacation!

All-inclusives are the best option because they free your mind from one of its top concerns: money. By not worrying about the price of a meal, drink, or activity, you can truly enter the vacation mindset. And by reading the following pages, I'll show you how to get the most out of every day of your trip.

In the last decade, my wife Beth and I have ventured on eighteen all-inclusive vacations. Any time our friends and coworkers consider taking a trip, they come to us for advice. We've experienced a variety of resorts and know exactly what to look for while planning. We've learned how to save money and most importantly, we've learned what to avoid.

Our first all-inclusive trip which was our honeymoon, was filled with a lot of questions and rookie mistakes. Why are there a dozen different people claiming to be our ride from the airport? Is it safe to leave our resort for a day trip? What surprise costs are not included in an all-inclusive? Do we need to tip just to get service? How do we get the most for our money? And of course...Why shouldn't we do shots with strangers?

Booking a trip without any guidance will result in putting you and your money in danger. We used to use travel agents until we learned how they guide you to resorts based on what equates to a commission for them. Another time we accidentally booked a trip that coincided with a college class I was taking. We even gambled on fate by ignoring trip insurance. The vacation industry is massive, but with this book's advice, you can make sure the money you spend is focused on you, not the people who are there to supposedly help.

Chapter 2
Choosing the Best Resort for Your Money

Some of the resorts are worth returning to year after year, while others, despite seeming great at the time, failed to earn our encore visit. One size does not fit all, so use this guide to find out what you should look for in a resort so you can avoid a week-long nightmare.

They all look like paradise over the internet, but much like online dating, a lot of them are hiding some disturbing issues. Online reviews are very helpful, but there are other less subjective factors to consider.

What are the best ways to save money when booking an all-inclusive vacation?

The first major factor to consider is whether you can get a direct flight to your destination. This saves precious vacation hours as well as hundreds of dollars. Different vacation companies have direct flights out of different cities, so shop around. Search until you find a package that offers a direct flight. We're fortunate in that St. Louis flies direct chartered flights to numerous resorts in Mexico as well as Punta Cana in the Dominican Republic. When we flew to Costa Rica, we spent half of the morning sitting in Atlanta's airport. The connecting flights add several hundred dollars of cost to each traveler. With a direct flight, you not only save money, you might be able to have your toes in the ocean before noon.

Another method a lot of travel companies offer is letting the company pick the resort for you. You'll select the features of a resort you're looking for, such as adults only and the area you want to stay, and then the website will show you several options that it will select from. You'll be placed in a resort 2-6 weeks before your actual travel day. We've never tried this, but some friends told us it saved up to $800 per person. The only drawback is that it may place you at a resort you've already visited instead of a new adventure.

If you choose this option, be sure to read the reviews of all of the potential resorts you might be placed in. If any of them worry you, don't roll the dice.

When are the cheapest months to travel?

It's no secret which times of year are the busiest and therefore most expensive: spring break, winter holidays, and early summer. September and October, aka hurricane season, is often the most affordable. The resorts aren't nearly as populated either. We used to travel the second week of May before I became a full-time teacher. The resort population was just busy enough, but not too tranquil.

The day of the week that you fly alters the price as well. Some years we vacation from Thursday to Thursday and save close to a hundred dollars compared to trips that travel on the weekend.

When I'm planning on booking our vacation, I check the travel sites every day. It's amazing how the prices fluctuate through the various weeks. I also notice that after we book, the price goes down the next day. Some companies will refund you the difference, so be sure to ask them about that policy. One trip, we were refunded $200 because of a sale price that didn't start until the following week.

Proximity to the airport

Another detail to research is how far away your resort is from the airport. Even if you're on a week-long trip, you don't want to waste an entire day traveling to the resort. Cancun's highway leads down a strip of resorts that are all located within an hour. At Costa Rica, it took almost two hours on bumpy back roads to reach our destination. The highway systems are not the same as in the United States, so even fifty miles can take close to two hours. To check ahead of time, just use Google Maps from the airport where you'll be landing.

A friend of mine stayed at a resort in Tulum after landing in Cancun. He said they arrived around four hours after the flight landed. The drive from the airport took longer than his flight from the United States!

Adults only

Another factor to consider is whether you're taking a family trip or going child-free. In 2013 my wife Beth and I visited our first adults-only resort. This is now a must for us. No offense parents, but unless you're bringing your kids along, find a place sans children for a more enjoyable experience. There's nothing worse than having to wait at the swim-up bar because little Trevor and his brother need another round of Shirley Temples. My wife was friendly to a child at a swim-up bar in Mazatlán, and by the end of the week we were hiding from him because he wouldn't leave us alone. He wanted nothing to do with his siblings, and we couldn't find his parents. Kids are okay in small doses, but we didn't take the trip to babysit someone else's.

Small children and even teenagers who are legally allowed to drink at a much younger age tend to ruin the romantic mood at dinner as well, and I don't think I need to remind anyone of their etiquette at breakfast and lunch buffets. I don't hate children (I'm a high school teacher), but there are certain situations in life when it's pleasant not to have any around.

I've also discovered that some resorts attract an older crowd. As I write this, I'm in my early 40s. A resort we visited in March made us feel young. The resort we vacationed at in July made us wish we were *still* young. Online reviews and social media accounts of these resorts will clue you in on whether there's a party atmosphere or not. Larger resorts tend to attract a younger crowd and more groups. Adults-only does not mean it isn't a party resort, so if you're into that, go for it. If you're looking for a more mellow and romantic vibe, search for a smaller resort. The quickest way to distinguish a resort's capacity is the size of its pools. Investigate the pictures on websites like Travelocity for best results.

Luxury versus budget

It's understandable that everyone is on their own budget, and no one likes saving a buck more than me. Still, there are luxuries well worth the extra cost. In 2015, we booked a spring break trip for 10 days in Mazatlán, Mexico for under $3,000 for both of us. It was all-inclusive, but not adults-only. A great value, but not without flaws. This section will compare the differences so you can decide on what fits your tastes and what you can tolerate.

Upon check-in, there are many resorts that will snap a bright-colored band around your wrist for the entire trip. It's an easy way to make sure no one sneaks in and mooches for free. This can happen when resorts are too close to each other. Classier resorts, often isolated on their own beach, won't require you to wear a plastic bracelet all week which I find beneficial, especially during pictures.

Towel cards are another inconvenience at value resorts. During check-in, you get one card per guest to give to the towel guy down at the pool or beach. At the end of the day, you exchange your dirty towels for cards. So what happens if someone steals your towel during the day? We were told we would need to pay $30 to replace it. My wife got us around this by pulling a dirty towel out of a bin while I distracted the towel guy. Unless you keep a close eye on your towel, someone who lost his or hers might take yours. At the adults-only resorts, we've never dealt with towel cards. They trust the guests to take only as many as they need.

One of the worst value-resort horror stories I've heard was shared with me by a friend's honeymoon experience. Even though the resort was all-inclusive, none of the bartenders poured drinks unless the guest had cash in hand ready to tip. Tipping will be discussed later, and while I do tip bartenders, it should not be necessary just to get service. Otherwise, you're still paying for drinks on a tab you already settled up when you booked the trip. Again, I'm for tipping, but not every drink (or I'd be broke by day two).

Be sure to check the number of restaurants and bars at your resort. Value resorts will only have one to three dinner options which will become very repetitive over the course of a week. There should be at least four or more dining options during your stay. Another nuisance is having to make dinner reservations for the resort's restaurants. Many resorts require you to stand in line at the concierge to reserve your spot the morning of your planned dinner. You should be relaxing, not waiting in a line. Reservations also obligate you to be ready at a certain time which conflicts with the whole theme of vacation of doing things on your own whimsical schedule.

On our honeymoon, we were given a punch card which allowed us to visit each restaurant only once. For the amount of money you're spending, you should have the freedom to have the same choices every night.

Premium liquor and beer are also more readily available at a luxury resort. Consuming cheap beer, off-brand liquor, and low-quality wine only increases your chance of a hangover. As you get older, you can't underestimate the importance of higher-quality drinks.

The point is, for around $300 to $500 more on average, you can take a vacation with no wristbands, no towel cards, no dinner reservations, no need for excessive tipping, and no children. There are other bonuses as well. Along with the above, most luxury resorts now offer free room service 24 hours a day. A value resort still might have room service, but it comes with a price. The luxury of having late-night food delivered to your door at no additional cost is a true blessing.

What if we're bringing our children?

There are luxury resorts that are still family-friendly. These resorts even have special pools and water playgrounds for the younger guests as well as additional activities. You and your partner can frequent the swim-up bar while your offspring hang out with the kids-club staff. Check reviews to see which resorts people trusted the staff to entertain their children.

Are online reviews reliable?

Some resorts have several thousand online reviews. If there aren't at least several hundred, they may not be reliable. A trusty average should accumulate from so many ratings. Even if a resort has a high average, I like to check a number of the negative reviews to see what happened. Often times they're isolated incidents with accusations of something wrong with a particular room. Room problems are going to happen from time to time, but it's how the resort addresses it that matters. In the more positive reviews you'll often hear people complimenting how the resort compensated for whatever problems a guest was having. If there's a consistency (bugs, food poisoning, bad service, faulty AC, etc.), you should consider a different resort.

It's important to read reviews from the previous year on the week you're planning to vacation. For example, if you're going to book your trip for the first week of August, scroll back through the reviews to read what the resort was like that particular week in the previous year. Was it overcrowded? Is it part of the rainy season? Certain countries do have a rainy season (especially Costa Rica and other countries around Central America), so carefully research before booking. We take trips mid-March and mid-July and have never had much rain aside from the occasional small shower. Good or bad, people will mention the weather in their reviews.

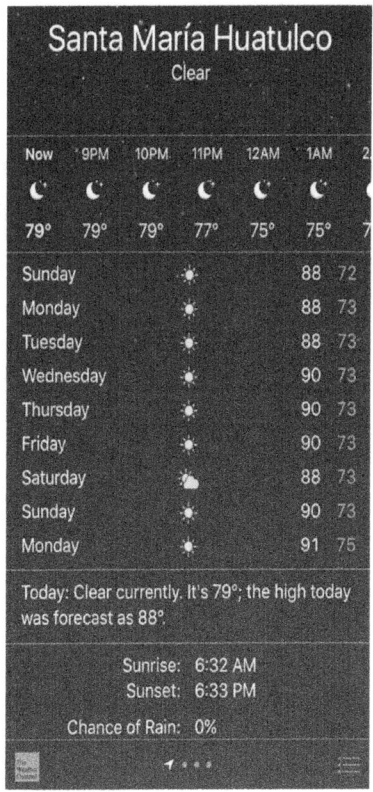

What should we know about the weather?

Certain countries have rainy seasons which will severely damper your week. For example, Costa Rica's rainy season (May to mid-November) is when the nature-lovers normally visit. Instead of swim-up bars, they're out exploring the forests which are finally green and full of life. The times we've visited (both in the spring), the foliage was mostly brown and there wasn't a drop of rain all week.

In the Caribbean, you might experience a brief shower on multiple afternoons. These are visible as they approach from the horizon, but they only last for maybe twenty minutes. A lot of people never even leave the pool. All of our travels have fallen between March and July, and we've never experienced rain more than twice in a week.

It's no secret that late August and all of September is hurricane season in the Atlantic. Trip insurance is a must!

Should we buy trip insurance?

Yes! Normally it's around $100 a person, but it's well worth it. Trip insurance allows you to cancel the otherwise, non-refundable parts of your trip due to illness/injury, a death in the family, hurricanes, or even work emergencies. Most cover several other reasons as well.

When I accidentally booked our honeymoon over the first week of a college class, we paid $500 to move the trip one week earlier because we didn't have insurance. Fortunately, the cost of the trip that week was $800 less so we were blessed to actually gain $300 back. This is another example of how much a price can fluctuate based on the week you travel.

Aside from cancellations, an even more valuable benefit is medical coverage. Your health insurance may not extend outside of the United States, and you don't want to deal with billing from a third-world country (a Q-tip is $8 at Cancun's hospital).

Trip insurance also covers lost luggage and flight delays should you have to spend another night at a hotel. You don't want to spend the night sleeping in a foreign terminal.

These are only a few of the benefits that provide peace of mind for your upcoming trip. Vacation is about removing stress from your life, so buy the trip insurance just in case. If you can't afford the extra cost, you're gambling thousands of dollars.

Is last-minute booking a good idea?

Yes, but there's a catch. Resorts will definitely drop prices on the weeks that aren't as busy which will occur during the school year. It's not a good idea to try last-minute anything for spring break. The problem is that flights will fill up before the resort. If you can't get a direct flight, you lose precious time on your travel days, and it's going to cost more. However, we've met people in the summer who paid much less than us by booking only a week or two out. It's a tricky gamble if you're up for the risk. If you already have the flight booked, go for it.

What are some reasons why I shouldn't go to an all-inclusive?

I wouldn't suggest taking a trip that puts you into debt. Save up for a year instead of charging that much money on something that will take months or years to pay off. If you're fortunate enough to get a tax refund, that's a great foundation to start saving.

Somehow paradise isn't for everyone. If you read the online resort reviews, you'll see multiple complaints at even the highest rated resorts. If you're overly sensitive to heat and different foods, but insensitive to different cultures, stay home. When you're in a different country, sometimes service requires a little more patience. For example, in the Dominican Republic they refer to the "Dominican five minutes" which is closer to fifteen.

The workers at these resorts are paid a lot less than they would be at a similar style of resort in the U.S. They're doing their best, but if you go in with a biased opinion, you and your "I need to speak to a manager" attitude shouldn't leave the country.

You'll also encounter travelers from other continents. Their cultural norms are not the same as those in the United States, so you might have to adjust to those differences as well. For example, swimwear.

Inevitably, we always see some old man snapping his fingers at a server and yelling, "Hey hombre!" You give your country a bad reputation when you do that. I don't know how many times I've apologized on behalf of the rest of us Americans, but sadly not everyone is respectful.

What other expenses are there?

The price you see for an all-inclusive is just the starting point. There are other expenses to consider. Obviously, you need a passport which will cost you over $100 and possibly take a couple months, so don't procrastinate that task.

Some airlines will charge baggage or even seating fees, so consider those ahead of time. Once you land, certain countries have entrance or exit fees. Mexico currently doesn't, but Costa Rica charged us $25 per person to leave. The Dominican Republic has a small fee too.

You'll probably want to take at least one day trip which can run anywhere from $25 to $200 a person. Every resort has a spa which will be heavily promoted for massages and other services. Some of the restaurants will offer menus with fancier foods like lobster for additional costs. And though free wine is offered, it's normally cheap South American red or white, so you have the option of buying a finer bottle at dinner. Souvenirs and tipping round out the other expenses you need to budget for. All of the above will be broken down further so that you can make the best decisions on where your money goes.

What if I can't speak Spanish?

Speaking Spanish is not mandatory. You'll notice at the resort, the more fluently someone speaks English, the higher the position they hold. Bartenders, tour guides, concierges, activity directors, and anyone in sales will understand you. Servers and food runners normally have a strong grasp, though sometimes a phrase may get lost in translation. Housekeeping and landscapers may not be able to have a conversation with you. Understand that you're in a foreign country where English is not the first language, so unless you know Spanish, you'll need to be patient and understanding with everyone.

Over the years my Spanish from high school and college has become rusty, but I know enough to take care of the basics. On our last trip, I even corrected the bellman on our room number using Spanish numbers. Most people know the basics: El baño, cerveza, gracias, etc.

Most of the television channels will be in Spanish too. However, a lot of the movies are in English with Spanish subtitles. Television shouldn't be one of your main activities anyway, so don't worry about it.

Menus at the restaurant and daily schedules of activities will also have English translations. They aren't perfect, but you'll be able to figure out what they're saying, despite some odd phrasing.

If you're still concerned, there are smartphone apps such as "Say Hi" that translate for you.

Language mishaps lead to some of the funniest moments. For example, one year in Mexico we were enjoying an outdoor Mexican fiesta night at a table with other couples. The post-dinner show began and included a routine of fire baton-twirling. The routine's soundtrack? "Smack My Bitch Up" by Prodigy. The whole table had a good laugh about it while the show's producer probably didn't consider the song's meaning. Another time, the DJ at a pool played the song, "F--- It, I Don't Want You Back" which drops the f-bomb at least two dozen times. Fortunately, this was an adults-only resort.

I've had my share of messing up Spanish. The Mexican people are understanding and patient, so you should be the same. Either way, you can usually tell what someone is trying to say.

Are group trips a good idea?

We've pulled this off once. There was a group of five other friends who joined us for the last five days of a ten-day trip. The friend who went stag actually met his future wife on the beach that week. We arrived from different cities, so everyone was in charge of their own logistical issues, but there weren't any major problems. If you stagger your arrival and departure dates, you gain the advantage of some alone time with your significant other. I also notified the resort a month ahead of time, so they were able to put our rooms near each other.

Consider the behavior of the other couples you'll be drinking with. Will they be fighting or need you to babysit them? If so, leave them behind. If you do all go as a group, establish a sufficient amount of exclusive time with your significant other.

Another challenge with a group is getting everyone to dinner on time. At most resort restaurants they'll either need a reservation or everyone there on time for large groups to sit together.

Realize that everyone has different priorities on vacation, so don't try to schedule how your pals spend the day. If they sleep in or pass out early, that's their prerogative. You can only control how your time is spent.

I would recommend everyone take a day trip adventure together. Sometimes you can negotiate a group discount if you book ahead of time. Book it beforehand to get the logistics out of the way.

Chapter 3
Preparing for Your Trip

Aside from the obvious, what else should I pack?

Almost every resort requires men to wear khaki or dress pants for dinner at their restaurants. If you're eating at the buffet it won't matter, but you don't want to miss out on the better menus. Jeans may not cut it, especially those with stylish holes. Along with nice pants, men also have to wear a collared shirt at dinner, so bring plenty of those unless you want to get stuck at the buffet every night. The resort's website will specify the dress code. This is taken seriously, so pay attention to it.

Packaged snacks are great for the trip. Travel days can be expensive if you choose airport food, so a small pouch of whatever you like can suffice. Customs will ask you if you're transporting any food in or out of the country, but these don't count, so tell them no. Customs is more concerned with raw meats, nuts, fruits, and other natural foods that could be infected.

We don't have a selfie-stick, but sometimes we bring our tripod to take pictures of ourselves before dinner, though it's never difficult to find someone to snap a couples photo for you.

Book collections at resorts are normally low-quality romance novels, often in Spanish, so make sure you bring your own reading material. Wi-Fi can be shoddy, so load plenty of reading ahead of time.

Don't forget the chargers for your phone, e-reader, camera, etc. Remember, you cannot fly with lithium ion batteries, so leave those at home.

Bring at least two pairs of sunglasses. My wife once lost hers to a wave on day one. Luckily she had replacements, because, like everything else, the gift shop is overpriced. I bring at least three pairs of swim trunks as well, because one or two are always drying out.

The toilet paper quality at most resorts is adequate, but with the potential for extra visits because of stomach issues and the risk of them cutting costs with cheaper TP, you can always play it safe and bring your own roll.

We've battled a few colds during vacation, so cold medicine always comes with us. They have it in the gift shops too, but it's expensive and not as effective.

If you have any allergies, don't forget to pack whatever you need to combat those. Also, a bottle of aspirin is a must! You never know what aches and pains will pop up.

What should I leave behind?

Due to baggage standards of around fifty pounds per suitcase, minimize your heavier objects (shoes, thicker books, etc.). You don't need to bring any alcohol of your own. Flotation devices aren't necessary either. They're a pain when the pool is crowded, and a lot of resorts have foam floaters in the pool every morning. You don't need to pack any towels because the resort has you covered.

Should I exchange my currency?

Unless you plan on exploring the country independently, it really isn't necessary. Everything at the resort can be paid for with American cash or credit card. Your credit card company will calculate the exchange rate for you (with a very small fee), but it's safer than worrying about pesos or other foreign currency. Find out what the exchange rate is, and if you're going to shop a lot, make a cheat sheet. The gift shops usually list cost in pesos, so using the sheet or by calculating on your phone, you can figure out how much you're actually spending.

The staff members at the resort actually prefer the American dollar in most countries because it's a lot more stable than their currency. Their banks will always accept it. Plus, it gives you a better idea of how much money you're spending on everything.

How do I get in shape for my trip?

Feel free to skip this part if you're not concerned.

When I met my wife, she was a fitness instructor. She takes her health and fitness very seriously, which has rubbed off on me over the years. She's taught me how to prepare for the trips. Is there anything beyond simple vanity to motivate a person to diet and exercise? Yes, there's another bonus. By restricting your diet in the months leading up to your vacation, all of the food tastes ten times better when you finally indulge. Everyone looks forward to the beach, the relaxation, and getting away from work, but oddly enough, I've found myself using the phrase, "I just can't wait to have a sandwich!" in my anticipation. If you've dieted before, you understand what I mean.

If you're planning for a honeymoon, maybe you want to be in the best shape of your adult life anyway. After all, you're probably going to pay a lot of money for a photographer.

Legally, I'll tell you to consult your physician before beginning any diet and exercise program. I'm just going to share what works best for me. It may take you more or less time and effort, depending on body type and age.

Though I lift weights year-round, I try to increase my workouts ten weeks out from the trip. I make it a priority, which often cuts into a lot of other activities in life. You have to decide whether it's worth it. It's an easy decision on day one, but by the end of week two you'll see just how honest with yourself you actually are. Find workouts that burn fat and build muscle—they're all over the internet. Six-minute ab videos are in abundance on YouTube.

I spend less time discussing the exercise portion because that's not the major factor. I believe diet dictates around 90% of success or failure. If you're working out just so you can eat junk food later on that night and supposedly break even, you won't make any progress.

There have been years where I was motivated to work out in the mornings, but as a teacher, I usually delay exercise until after school. Following each workout, I take in around 40 grams of protein with a shake. These can be pricey, but they motivate me to make the most of my time in the gym.

For the highest chance of success, make it a joint effort with whoever you're vacationing with. If you live together already, you can hold each other accountable and rid your kitchen of all its junk food.

Know that any day that you drink alcohol will result in not losing weight. I'm not suggesting you go ten weeks without a drop and then head to a week-long open bar at your resort (don't do that!). I suggest that you spend the first month of the program dry. For our March trip, this equates to a dry January. If you need a month not to drink, January is the most common choice.

I'm not a dietician, but here's what works for me: low sugar, high protein. If you can limit your sugar (which includes carbs) to around 30 grams a day, you're going to lose weight quickly. After only a couple weeks, you'll notice your food and drink tasting differently. When I'm not dieting, my protein shake has zero sweetness no matter what flavor I choose; however, in the midst of my diet, it tastes like the world's best milkshake. This works with other foods as well. Diet foods are an acquired taste that become easier on the palate.

I start my day with a bowl of oatmeal with almond milk because regular milk is filled with sugar. Getting your carbs in early and naturally will give you just enough energy to survive the day. I add either blueberries or protein powder for flavor. I drink my coffee black and avoid sugars and creamers. Artificial sweeteners only trigger cravings, so don't fall for that trap.

A handful of almonds, a sweet potato, or a small piece of fruit works as a mid-morning snack. You don't need to starve yourself. For lunch, I eat a salad made of spring mix. I add more almonds, banana peppers, and sometimes a can of tuna. Check your dressing for sugar content. The point of eating a salad is lost if you choose the wrong dressing. Fat-free dressing is going to contain more sugar, so just choose a vinaigrette or make your own out of vinegar and extra-virgin olive oil.

Caramel-flavored rice cakes with a touch of low-sugar peanut butter are a go-to during my afternoons. They may not seem appetizing in week one, but once your taste buds adapt, they taste like a dessert.

Dinners risk becoming rather monotonous. Fat-free turkey, whole wheat pasta salad, salmon, fat-free refried beans, and eggs (1 to 2 yolks, and then egg whites scrambled) usually rotate on my menu. Broccoli accompanies whatever I choose most nights.

Seasonings can add extra sugar and salt to your body, so I suggest hot sauce. Sodium is high in hot sauces, but usually they're sugar-free and add enough kick.

Then there's evening. This is what separates success from failure. It's not nearly as challenging to stay disciplined throughout your busy day, but once you sit back and turn on the television, your stomach is going to tell you it's hungry. Advertisements for all of the foods you have to avoid are going to air over and over. If you're youthful enough to postpone your workouts until this late, perhaps you can try that instead of relaxing. Personally, I don't have the energy or motivation by this point in the day, and I can't go to bed hungry. Here's what I suggest for an evening snack: fat-free Greek yogurt with protein powder or blueberries. Again, it's not going to taste good early on, but eventually you'll learn to enjoy it. The hours from dinner to bedtime will make or break your results.

Once a week, my wife and I will eat a cheat meal, but we don't go crazy on it either. Homemade pizza with a store-bought wheat crust is our usual pick. Our toppings include mushrooms, banana peppers, and fat free mozzarella cheese (it's a thing), all with a low-sugar traditional sauce.

If you're struggling with hunger, find foods with healthy fats. Salmon, avocados, and almonds can quell stomach growling.

Other than slimming down and walking around the pool with confidence, there are other benefits to this diet. I notice that, during the last month leading up to the trip, I need less sleep. I spend less time in the bathroom and feel healthier overall. It takes a lot of willpower, but eventually you can get used to it. If it's your body's first diet, it will have an even greater impact. It does take patience, maybe even six weeks to notice a marginal difference, but once you gain momentum, it's very rewarding to experience results.

Preparing for travel day

My wife and I don't have a house sitter, so we make a checklist of everything that needs to be done leading up to and including the morning of our departure. We put our mail on hold using the USPS website. We also adjust our thermostat, turn off our water, set a timer on our lights, change our voicemail greetings, and set up any necessary away messages on email. If you don't trust the people on your social media, don't announce your trip (and empty house) ahead of time.

Decide which credit or debit cards you're taking and notify the company that you're leaving the country. Sometimes an international purchase can trigger a fraud alert and shut your credit card down.

The most important thing to keep track of is your passport. You don't need any other form of identification. Remove gift cards and extra credit cards from your wallet, so they can remain safely at home. It's a good idea to make a paper copy of your passport to keep with you just in case. You'll need to keep your passport handy during the flight as well, because there is an immigration form to fill out while you're in the sky.

One thing we've altered over the years is our method of transportation to the airport. Fortunately, we live only a short distance away, so cab rides aren't that expensive. Parking and using a shuttle can be troublesome with the amount of luggage you might have. I trust you'll arrive at the airport cautiously early. Most international flights want you to check-in around two hours before takeoff even if you have a connecting flight before leaving the country. My wife and I reward ourselves after getting through security in plenty of time by getting an early-morning drink near our gate. No judgment, it's vacation!

What paperwork is needed to leave the country?

Other than your passports and boarding passes, you should keep a copy of your hotel information with you. On the flight to a foreign country, you'll be given an immigration form to fill out before you land. Having this slip filled out properly will get you through customs quicker. Be sure to have a pen handy because the flight attendants won't have enough. The slip only needs basic information such as your name, destination, flight number, passport number, and date of birth. I mention date of birth last because a lot of people mess that one up. Other countries list the day before the month, so pay attention when filling that part in.

When you go through customs, they'll stamp your passport, tear the top part of your immigration form off for their records, and give you the bottom part stamped. Do not lose this half-sheet! It could cost hundreds of dollars to replace. You will need it on your way home, so keep it clipped to the pages of your passport.

How do I get from the airport to my hotel?

Most vacation packages include a free shuttle transfer from the airport to the resort. If you rented a car or are taking your chances with a cab, you can skip this section.

Once you get through customs and claim your luggage, you'll walk through what I can only describe as a gauntlet of offers. Most airports, especially Cancun, have a corridor of counters for rental cars, day trips, and timeshares. Ignore everyone in this hallway! They will try and act like you're supposed to go with them. They sometimes look at the vacation company tag on your luggage and pretend to be with that company. Keep your eyes on the doorway, and once outside you should be able to find your trip's representative to direct you to either a van or bus to shuttle you to your resort. They usually have a sign and a special shirt.

Waiting on your shuttle takes a little patience, because not everyone gets through the airport as quickly. Some people buy (very overpriced) drinks for the ride there. Some get stuck in gift shops. Others might be waiting on luggage. We usually have to wait around twenty minutes before the shuttle finally gets us out of the airport. Another annoying issue is that sometimes your shuttle will stop and drop people off at other resorts. This doesn't always happen, but it depends on whose resort is closer and how many people from your flight are headed to the same resort as you.

Your representative will give you information on the ride there. Some of it is interesting information about the area, but most of it is to promote day trips. Usually this person will be stationed at your hotel to help you with any other questions. They'll arrange a meeting time either that afternoon or the following morning to give you more information.

The shuttle ride to the resort is often an eye-opener. If you've never been to that part of the world before, the poverty you'll witness can be shocking. Even the livestock appear starved. My first time to Costa Rica, I had a sense of guilt the first few days, because while I was enjoying a paradise, the workers were trying to make ends meet. I justify it because I'm helping tourism, the country's most valuable industry.

Chapter 4
Welcome to the Good Life!

What's the check-in process like?

You'll be checking in at the same time as everyone else on your shuttle, so the first thing you should do is identify your luggage as it comes off the vehicle. I always tip the driver a couple of bucks, too. If you sit in the front of the shuttle, you can get in line first.

Be sure you have all of your important paperwork with you. The guide on your shuttle will give you a voucher for next week's shuttle trip back to the airport on that day. Keep it with your passport and immigration form.

Most resorts have a wonderful greeting as you walk in. A cool, wet towel to wipe down with and a small glass of champagne or a mini-beer is pretty standard at the finer resorts. Don't be surprised if the Dominican Republic resorts offer you a shot of their mamajuana. It's their trademark liquor and holds a unique flavor.

While checking in, they'll cover the basics and offer a room upgrade. Negotiating upgrades is possible at many of the resorts. They'll give you a price, but feel free to counter. It depends on the resort and the availability.

Once you're done checking in, make sure your passports and other valuables are secure. At this point you still won't have a room key—you won't be able to move into your room until around 3:00. Plan ahead and carry a backpack with your valuables and everything else you might need, such as a swimsuit and other necessary items if you want to go swimming before your move-in time. If you forget, the rest of your luggage is normally stored in a room near the lobby. Ask at the front desk for access.

The time before you move into your room is a great opportunity to relax and enjoy your first meal. The staff will show you where you can eat lunch. Avoid getting tipsy too early on day one, at least until you have your room available to you.

How can I acquire the best room for my price range?

Some resorts have a quieter side compared to a party side. If you're a night owl, take the party side. Otherwise, you're going to hear doors opening and closing earlier in the morning. If you figure on going to bed at a decent hour, you're going to want the side away from the dance club and nightlife, or even the potential wedding reception that might last past midnight.

Some resorts consist of many smaller buildings of only three floors. I advise taking the top floor if possible, because sometimes guests or housekeepers move furniture around at strange hours. You don't want to be woken up from an afternoon nap by the people upstairs. It's worth the inconvenience of taking the elevator or stairs every trip.

You can't always get your room preference, especially if you're not upgrading, because of availability. However, a trick I learned is to contact the hotel via social media months ahead of time with your reservation number. My wife and I had room 55 on our honeymoon in Punta Cana. I remembered it as a perfect location in a rather large resort. When we returned for our 5-year anniversary, I requested room 55 again about a month before our trip. They were able to make it happen.

Some resorts, depending on the country, still have hallways or buildings where smoking is permitted. These tend to be louder because people spend a lot of time on their balconies. If you're a smoker, email and ask about this ahead of time. Otherwise, assume you're in a non-smoking area.

If your room has a major problem, the resort should be able to accommodate you promptly. We met a couple who had a room near a pile of bulldozed seaweed close to the resort. They complained about the smell and were upgraded to a large suite at no extra cost.

Are the upgrades worth it?

In my opinion, they're not worth it. There's enough space in a standard-sized room. We don't spend much time in our room; it's mainly for sleeping or getting ready for dinner. Only once did we ever choose an upgraded room (our travel agent chose it for us somehow), and there wasn't a huge difference. There was a small Jacuzzi on the balcony, but I think I only used it once; it felt silly being on display and near other balconies.

Choosing an upgraded room might make you a target for other additional services that cost extra. Still, if you have the disposable income for the upgrade, go for it. The most noticeable difference to consider when deciding on an upgrade is the privacy of the bathroom (see page 33, "What's up with the bathroom?").

Do we have to go to the orientation meeting?

Technically, no. It's not a bad idea if it's your first trip, or if you're new to the resort, but we haven't attended one in years. The main purpose of the meeting is to try and sell day trips. Other than that, it covers hotel basics like reservations, amenities, and activities, but you can figure those out on your own by reading the rest of this book. The meetings typically last at least a half-hour and they don't start on time.

What is the biggest time-wasting trap?

Nothing will ruin your day like wasting hours on a timeshare presentation. No matter how short they promise it will run, do not attend it. They'll offer you spa dollars and day trips, but you should still decline. If you've never experienced a timeshare presentation, it's hard to describe just how frustrating they become. My wife and I were suckered into one on our second trip, and it was four hours we'll never get back, and that's when we cut it short. These people are trained never to take no for an answer and will keep you for as long as they can.

Timeshare presentations often take you away from the resort, so you have no means of bailing on them early. The spa dollars can only be used in small increments, so you still have to spend money there. Timeshare representatives use sales techniques that make used car dealers look honest. Trust me, it is not worth the so-called reward.

Other resorts offer VIP, Vacation Clubs and Privilege memberships as well. These usually involve a room upgrade, access to better liquor, access to a special lounge, and spa discounts. They come at a hefty price (19 grand where we stayed last year, but I've heard other resorts charging 6 figures). In my opinion, they are not worth it.

These sales reps speak English as well as any American and have their techniques down to a science. They know how to manipulate you into signing a deal. They start as overly friendly, but they're actually calculating their method of potential sales.

What's up with the bathroom?

One of the most noticeable things about all-inclusive hotels is their complete disregard for privacy in the bathroom, especially at the basic room level. Often there is no actual bathroom door, only a fogged-glass divider for a toilet stall. Bathrooms are normally tucked around the corner from the sleeping area, but they're definitely a little too close for comfort. So if you and your partner are not the type to leave the door open at home, you may want to consider a game plan for bathroom time. Happy honeymooning!

Can we drink the water from the faucet?

Definitely not! A few spots in Mexico claim that it's okay, but I wouldn't risk it. You can brush your teeth with tap water, but do not ingest it. The resort will use filtered water for ice, meals, and all other drinks, so you don't need to worry. Stock up on the resort's bottled water. Sometimes I visit the fitness center just to grab a few extra bottles.

What's in the fridge?

At every resort we've stayed, there's a mini-fridge with soda, water, juice, and whatever beer is domestic to that country. They refill this daily, so if you have a preference, just let them know and they'll stock it to your liking. It's a good idea to keep a surplus of water in there because a lot of countries don't have safe tap water for drinking. Resorts that aren't all-inclusive will price-gouge you when they refill your refrigerator.

Are the rooms secure?

Every room has a small safe where you should store passports and other valuables. Be sure you and your partner can agree on a 4-digit code which you can use for every vacation. Make it something you'll remember even at your drunkest moment.

Housekeepers value their jobs, so you do not need to worry when they're cleaning your room. One time my wife misplaced a ring and the housekeeper found it for us without us even asking.

What is turn-down service?

Along with a daily cleaning, most resorts offer turn-down service while you're at dinner. We feel very pampered returning to the room and finding our bed made yet again. They'll tidy up your bathroom sink, straighten any messes, and leave mints on the pillow. This is usually when they'll restock your fridge and deliver the daily schedule of tomorrow's activities as well. One resort chain even offers incense to burn in the evenings.

What is TV in a different country like?

Most of the resorts offer at least one premium movie channel. While a lot of the stations are in Spanish, there are at least a few in English. Obviously, you're not there to watch television, but if you need something to fall asleep to, you should have enough of a selection. Most adults-only resorts have a Playboy Channel or something else pornographic, so if you're offended by that, check the channel listings on what to avoid. We have stayed at family-friendly resorts with the Playboy Channel, so parents beware.

How do you keep your room cool?

We've rarely had any problems with a room not getting cool enough. If they're equipped with a ceiling fan, make sure it is rotating the correct way (there's a switch on the actual fan they can click for you). A lot of times the thermostats are set in Celsius, so if you want a cooler room, try around 17 degrees, which is the low 60s in Fahrenheit. Adjust to your preference.

You'll notice a small ringing sound when you open the sliding door to your balcony or patio. It reminds you that your AC shuts off while the door is open. This might happen when your front door opens as well. It's merely a precaution the resorts use to save energy. If a sliding door is opened to 90-degree heat, they don't want their AC blasting for no reason. As soon as the door closes, another noise will signal you that it's turning back on.

What's the point of the balcony when it's so hot out?

Our balcony is rarely visited. Sometimes if I wake up early, I'll sit out there and read while my wife snoozes. However, it does have a few purposes. We like to leave our suits out to dry. Hanging them over the edge of the balcony looks bad and is frowned upon, so we usually cover the chairs.

If you have a camera and store it in your room all night, it will fog up for quite a while when you take it outside the next day. If your balcony is secure and isolated, you can store your camera in its case outside. When you're ready to head out, take it through your room quickly and get it back outside to avoid any lens fog.

Why are the light switches so confusing?

For some unknown reason, the lighting situation is one of the more baffling puzzles you'll encounter. Sometimes rooms have a master switch just inside the door, so that you can turn everything off when you leave (or turn everything on when you arrive). While you're sober, take a couple of minutes to figure out which switch turns on what. Some resorts even require you to insert your key card to a master switch to get anything to turn on.

I suggest leaving the light on above the toilet so that you can see where you're going in the middle of the night in your new home. Figure out the ceiling fan situation early as well.

What should we look for once we get situated?

After finally receiving access to your room around 3:00, be sure your luggage arrives. We made the mistake of dragging our luggage to our room by ourselves one year, and my wife will never let me forget it. It was quite the haul.

Make sure you keep your resort map handy. Even if the resort is smaller, it helps you get around. Not all of the workers are able to direct you due to language barriers. In other words, don't ask a landscaper where the Italian restaurant is. It's not his job to direct you, and he may not be able to.

The pool and ocean should be relatively easy to locate. If you're going to work out during the week, locating the gym isn't a bad idea either. Resorts have signs along the sidewalk. If your room isn't ready, exploring is a worthy use of time.

Most places have a main buffet for breakfast and lunch, and then another breakfast and lunch option closer to the beach, so be sure to locate those to figure out which one you favor.

What are the keys to a happy day one?

Have patience. If you've been dieting and abstaining from alcohol, be careful not to shock your system right away. You're in a different environment, and it's going to affect your body in ways you're not used to.

Relax and enjoy the scenery on that first day. After you unpack and eat, get down to the pool or the beach and just relax. You might struggle to find a chair to set your bag on because of your late arrival, but hopefully you can squeeze in somewhere.

Since you probably got up very early, don't plan on staying up late and overdoing it on that first night. Ease your liver back into your college drinking habits, and choose a restaurant for an early dinner.

Chapter 5
Avoiding Rookie Mistakes

Sunburn

It's easy to tell who the new guests are as opposed to the people who have been there for almost a week. Their skin tone gives it away. Do not risk sunburn. If you build a base tan before you arrive, you still won't be safe from the sun's rays at a tropical level. Even if you have hair, your scalp can burn. SPF 50 should be applied as often as necessary to every inch of your exposed skin. It's very easy to ignore skincare while you're drunk and having an interesting conversation with your partner or people you meet near the swim-up bar.

Pack more than enough sunscreen, because if you run out, you'll pay four times as much. One year I accidentally packed our sunscreen in my carry-on luggage, which then didn't make it through security. The gift shop sunscreen was over $30.

After-sun lotions can be soothing after a shower. If your skin feels warm, these provide a little relief while you're trying to fall asleep at night. Aloe vera is a well-known remedy as well.

A lot of people wear pool shirts. These are not a fashion faux pas, so don't be ashamed to protect your skin. Realize that your body is in a completely foreign environment and isn't suited for this type of climate in the long term. Note how even locals take the necessary precautions against the sunshine and heat.

Going barefoot

One drunken afternoon in Costa Rica, I decided to leave my pool chair to visit the ocean. My feet were wet as I ran across the sand and into the water. In Guanacaste, the beach is dark because of volcanic remnants, so the sand bakes even hotter than usual. In my stupidity, I forgot to take my flip-flops, so I actually burnt my feet on the return run back to the pool. Luckily, the resort had small wooden boards every ten yards for idiots like me to stop on. Still, in between each stop I suffered, while others chuckled at my mistake.

It seems like common sense, but you'd be surprised at the number of people who burn their feet. Pavement and wooden walkways reach dangerous temperatures, so be careful.

Phone and social media issues

Carry a beach bag with pockets to store your phone and other items that could get wet. Never put your phone in the pocket of your swim trunks. In fact, don't bring your phone near the edge of the pool. There can be a lot of partying and games going on around the pool during certain activities. If you absolutely must keep your phone with you, invest in one of those plastic bag protectors. They range from $10-$20 and claim to seal your phone from any water damage. Hours of heat can damage your phone, so keep it out of direct sunlight.

Once you boarded the plane you should have put your phone in airplane mode, and not just because they say so. Having your phone turned on puts you on an international plan that will probably cost extra, so keep it in airplane mode until you land back home. In airplane mode you still have access to Wi-Fi. Hopefully you changed your voicemail greeting before you left.

If you have an international plan and are able to place calls, have the courtesy not to talk on the phone at the beach or pool. Hearing someone's conversation is annoying enough in the airport; no one wants to deal with it while trying to relax by the water.

While most resorts are starting to improve their Wi-Fi, a vacation is a great time to practice disconnecting from your cellphone addiction. Yes, it's tempting to post how wonderful of a time you're having every five minutes while your friends back home suffer through their daily routines, but try to limit that. If you post something early in the day, you're going to be tempted to check on likes and comments. What I advise is limiting yourself to only having your phone around for pictures, and then handling the social media postings while you wait for your partner to get ready in the morning or before dinner.

CAUTION: Do not drunk post! Trust me on this one. Whatever you need to share can be delayed until morning when your judgment returns. Use the buddy system with your partner on this if you don't trust yourself.

I suggest waiting until you get home and carefully inspecting your pictures before you post them all at once. It's easy to overlook wardrobe malfunctions and bad angles when you only inspect on your phone.

Getting suckered into a purchase

On a day trip during our honeymoon, my wife and I visited a coffee plantation in the Dominican Republic. One of the products that the plantation sold was small bottles of coconut oil. The guide described how applying coconut oil and sunbathing for twenty minutes is a safe and accelerated method to build up a tan. He went on to explain that if sunburnt, applying the same oil relieves the skin right away and the painful red aftermath never happens. Like suckers at a 19th century medicine show, my wife and I bought a container and tried it out the next day. "I don't feel tan, and it's already been twenty minutes," I said. We did another twenty.

Of course we burnt. That afternoon we applied the same oily elixir to our sunburns and did nothing but ruin our clean sheets. It was painful.

If something sounds too good to be true, it is. Keep this in mind when buying any jewelry, cigars (they're not really Cuban!), clothing, etc. Agree on a price ahead of time for the total package. For example, you may find out that $10 to braid hair actually means $10 per braid. Anytime you stray from the resort, you're on your own as far as business dealings. There's isn't any customer protection. Your trips should be about your experiences, not the souvenirs. I don't think we've ever spent more than $25 on any particular item. Plus, on the way home you have to list everything you purchased and answer questions to customs about your souvenirs.

Befriending a clingy couple

While it can be interesting to meet other people from faraway places like England, Canada... or Iowa, some couples can become a little clingy. It's easy to talk for hours when you're drinking in a perfect environment, but be careful. Once you sober up, your new friends could turn out to have issues that weren't apparent during your first impression.

One year while drinking in the pool, my wife and I met a couple who were on our same flight. After a number of margaritas, we invited them to our home in the States for dinner later that week. On the morning of the flight home, we discovered they were already a drunken mess an hour before takeoff. They were even louder on the flight home as they continued their drinking. Luckily we were able to separate ourselves at customs, though I believe they already understood we had rescinded our invitation.

We've met a lot of wonderful people through the years whom I still keep in touch with on social media. Still, if you want enough time to focus on your own relationship, draw some boundaries and politely decline dinner invitations.

Chapter 6
Making the Most of Vacation

What should I know about drinking?

While I'm not a functioning alcoholic back at home, I'll admit that during these trips, I consume a lot. Most resort bars open at 10:00 in the morning, but you can order mimosas or coffee with Irish cream at breakfast. I take it that you know your limits and whether you will hopelessly drink past them when given the chance, but here is some advice about drinking to consider while at an all-inclusive resort...including why you shouldn't do shots with strangers.

The first precaution is that the drinks are stronger. You won't see precise measuring, so assume your cocktails are almost automatically doubles. When you're not worried about cost and the conditions are perfect, every drink goes down a lot easier. When the service around the pool and beach is on point, you'll always have a beverage in your hand. Therefore, you're going to be drunker than usual. The sun's effect magnifies this.

There are times when people come up and start talking to us while using our names, and we don't remember them from the day before. We call this swim-up bar amnesia. I don't know how many times I've introduced myself to someone who already knows my name and background from a conversation I don't remember. The important thing is, you'll probably never see any of these people ever again, so go ahead and wear that crazy outfit, enter that dance-off, or wail that karaoke tune!

Why shouldn't we do shots with strangers?

On my most recent vacation I chatted with a man from Chicago at the swim-up bar. My wife was getting along with his wife, so we continued to talk about various interests: Seinfeld episodes, the Chicago Bears, music, and our love for tequila. The bar wasn't busy that day, so as soon as we wanted something, it was poured. My new friend and I sampled several shots of tequila, and even though I felt fine while we continued to discuss this and that, I ended up very drunk. That night I wasn't able to get up from my nap, so I missed dinner.

You never know when you're going shot for shot with someone who can hold twice as much as you. While you're standing in water, it's easy to feel sober, but the intoxication can sneak up on you. This is why I suggest not doing shots with strangers. They'll order before you're ready, and if you're in an interesting conversation, it's easy to lose track. Keep it up and you'll do worse than just missing dinner.

What are some ways to avoid overdrinking?

Staying hydrated is vital. I recall one resort where the servers around the pool passed out bottles of water right before the bars opened. If you can space out your drinks with hydration, you'll last a lot longer, especially in the sun.

Another risk with day drinking is your amount of time in the sun. You may forget to reapply sunscreen or lose track of just how many hours you've been there. I've even seen people pass out in the shade for so long that they wake up in sunlight.

Depending on the resort, bartending skills can vary. Occasionally a drink will be mixed so poorly that you have to dispose of it. I encountered a bartender in the Dominican Republic who accidentally made a margarita with rum instead of tequila. It happens. As the week goes on, you'll learn who makes which drinks the best. At one of the resorts in Mexico we have visited five times, there was a swim-up bartender who was on the slower side and not that great at his job. During the following years he became a master and is even mentioned in quite a few positive online reviews. Usually your swim-up bartenders are going to be some of the quickest in the resort.

Make a plan with your partner or friends, and trust them when they cut you off. You've hit your limit. Some people are better at this than others. If you cannot control your drinking, an all-inclusive resort might be a dangerous place. The worst incident we ever saw was a woman who passed out and went underwater while her husband stood by in ignorance, waiting for his order. Luckily someone saved her life and the medics took her up to her room. Fifteen minutes later, her husband was back at the swim-up bar, leaving her alone. Be sure your partner and you have a plan to take care of each other.

When I exceed my limit, Beth has been known to pull a prank or two...

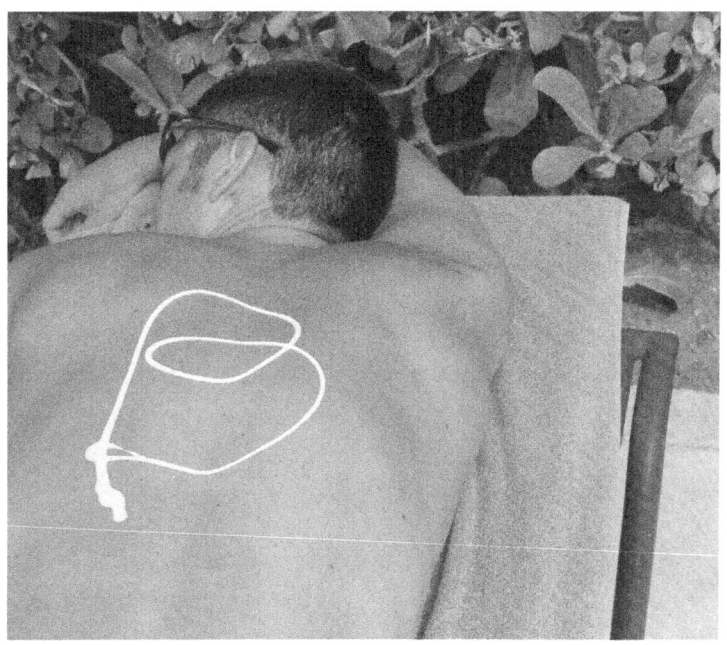

What is proper swim-up bar etiquette?

I can't imagine all of the obnoxious behavior bartenders endure. I've yet to go into details about tipping, but it's best to take care of your bartenders up front. First, wait until the bar actually opens before ordering—even if it's 10:01. Let the staff set up for the day; they're not on vacation. Second, limit your questions. There will be a waterproof menu available, but they can make all of the other standard drinks. If there are other people waiting, it's rude to order some drink that only the staff at your old college dive bar knows the recipe for. Also, if they aren't great at making a Manhattan, cut them some slack. It's a swim-up bar, not a piano lounge.

There are a lot of frozen drink options, including something called a Miami Vice. It's half daiquiri and half piña colada, so it's like making two drinks instead of one. If the bar is extremely slammed, stick to a simpler drink that only has one recipe. Even worse is the "stoplight," which is a red, yellow, and green mix. If you absolutely must order these, do it early on before there's a crowd.

More and more people are bringing their own mugs to the resort. I've heard from staff that they prefer you not do this. It may be harder to carry these monsters as they trudge through the sand while balancing the smaller cups. Also, you're more likely to drink past your limit when you use your own mug. Try using them for beer only. Guests claim that they're cleaner, but if you're reusing the same cup all afternoon, that may not be the case.

Most resorts are doing away with straws. Other countries are ahead of us environmentally, plus they're a lot closer to the sea turtles anyway, so don't expect straws. If you absolutely need one, they should have paper straws available, or you can always bring your own reusable straw.

If you're at a resort that includes children, please keep your little ones away from the swim-up bar. No one wants pool water splashed in their drink by nearby children. Also, the language and adult behavior on display there isn't something your offspring should witness anyway.

Drinking tips

Respect the bartender. If they want to knock you out in a couple of drinks, they'll pour it that way. They do not measure. With so many people clamoring (late afternoon swim-up bars are the busiest), be patient. If you're overlooked, it's not intentional. At the nicer resorts, they don't play favorites to the point of ignoring others.

Better resorts also use better liquors. You can request a certain type of tequila for your margarita if it's on the shelf. It's not uncommon to have unlimited access to a bottle that would cost over $40 in the States. These sometimes run out later in the afternoon, but if you can find them early, enjoy. I feel sorry for the people who refuse to venture out from cans of Bud Light. It's your chance to experiment at no extra cost. Take advantage!

Avoid the cocktails that contain a lot of lactose. If you drink the cream from piña coladas or mudslides all day, your stomach is going to let you know that was a mistake. You're already putting your system to the test by the amount of food and drink you're consuming; don't make it even more challenging.

Avoid getting salt on the rims of your margaritas. Too much salt will mess up your system, especially if you're dehydrated. Plus, your lips might get sunburnt. Adding salt (not to mention the salt from those fries at lunch) can lead to some painful burning. Lime juice from your drinks can make this even more painful.

Keep an eye on your partner or friends to make sure that they're pacing themselves and drinking enough water throughout the day. If you're going to be there for a week, it might be a good idea to take a day (or at least a morning and afternoon) off from drinking. This can coincide well with a day trip.

How are the fitness centers?

The fitness center at every resort reminds me of the first week of January back in the Midwest: It's amateur hour. You can spot the newly-determined exercisers by their extremely color-coordinated outfits. Vacation seems to give the New Year resolutions a second wind. The fitness center fills up later in the morning, so if you absolutely are determined to work out, rise with the sun. Fitness centers don't always have the best air conditioning, so by afternoon the room temperature might be intolerable.

If you don't work out at home, don't start on vacation. You're only going to plague yourself with sore muscles. We once witnessed a couple shuttled to the fitness center on a golf cart so that they could get on treadmills and walk. Again, if you don't workout at home, don't start on vacation.

If you work out like a health nut back at home, vacation can be a time to let your body rest. You'll be fairly active walking around the resort and swimming, but accept the fact that you're going to gain a few pounds. That's what vacations are for, right?

I attempt a half-assed version of my normal workout every two to three days. I know I feel better on the days that I exercise, but after training so hard to get in shape for the trip, it's refreshing to give the body (and the morning alarm) a break.

One trip, my wife and I worked out after our sobering afternoon naps. The gym was nearly empty every time, and it gave us more energy for the evenings. As a precaution, never work out while you're still drunk. Foreign treadmills are not forgiving!

What kind of wildlife lives around the resort?

One of my favorite features about traveling is encountering exotic animals. It's a welcome change from the usual batch of chipmunks, squirrels, and roadkill. The most notable resort animal is the standard iguana. These are abundant and range from one to four feet long. They won't bother you at all, and their movements are almost always relaxed. Occasionally you'll see one scamper across a sidewalk, but they're more common among the foliage.

Coatimundis are probably the only ornery animals around the resort. They tend to scavenge through any unattended food. They're raccoon-like, so don't attempt to pet them. They have long tails and can maneuver quickly, though they aren't dangerous to the average guest. Most resorts have signs instructing you not to feed them because they shouldn't ingest the carbs from human food. I've seen harmless packs of them as large as several dozens. Observe their cuteness and keep a few feet away, and you won't have any problems. However, if you have a ground-level patio and you leave food out, they will find it.

Gecko lizards are less noticeable, but show their presence at night. Sometimes they even crawl on the hallway walls or lights, though we've never had any enter our room. They dart quickly, but only add to the exotic aesthetics of your resort.

Birds tend to be a nuisance only during lunch hours. They'll swoop onto the outdoor tables when people leave behind a plate of scraps. I've seen even more aggressive birds steal from plates while someone was up getting a drink refill. I told the guy when he returned to his table, but he continued to eat from the same plate a bird had perched on. C'est la vie.

Servers are effective about keeping the birds away. We stayed at a resort that even kept a net over the tables at lunch. My favorite method for scaring off birds is when a resort has its own falcon (which we ignorantly nickname "El Birdo"). The "falcon guy" walks around the pool most days while his bird soars around the area with bells on his legs. These birds fascinate me, so I always visit the falcon guy to get a picture of "El Birdo" perched on my hand. He gets a generous tip for this.

What about bugs?

Mosquitos are only abundant at dawn and twilight. If you're dining outside for breakfast or dinner, you may want to spray yourself with repellant.

Bees are a problem at some resorts, but at the finer resorts, we haven't noticed them. They tend to collect at the swim-up bars where servers spill syrups and liquors. You can actually witness bees getting drunk. My wife got stung on her side in Costa Rica, and it left a mark for nearly a year, so if you're allergic, don't forget your emergency medicines. Read the resort's online reviews to see if bees are a problem there. Somehow the better resorts keep their swim-up bars bee-free.

Should we visit the spa?

I have a hunch that resort spas are how they make a lot of their profit. The basic services are usually listed in pesos (or whatever the country's currency is), so be sure you calculate how much you're going to pay. They're very expensive, but if you can afford it, that's up to you. We've splurged on massages before, though they're not anything special. One time the package included something called "hydro-therapy" which was almost laughably silly. A small group of us sat in a sauna, exited, and then experienced warm and cold water through different methods (wading pools, showers, etc.) for about a half-hour. It made no sense.

If you want a massage, sometimes you can find independent masseuses along the beach or in the nearby town. These are a terrific value. One time, my wife and I had a one-hour couples massage on the beach for only $60. To this day it's still the best massage I've ever received. Unfortunately, luxury resorts don't seem to have independent masseuses around, so your only option is the resort's spa.

You won't have a hard time booking anything, because the spa saleswoman (you can spot her lipstick from a mile away) makes rounds at the pool or beach and speaks English very well. Don't fall for the "one-day special" sales tactic. You can usually negotiate and haggle even on these services.

One year my wife had terrible back pain and purchased several massages. At the end of the week, they gave her a total that didn't match what she thought she owed. She was able to persuade them to adjust it to the price she agreed on.

What are mornings on the resort like?

If you never get to sleep in and need your vacation to do so, catch up on your sleep. However, if you can make it up in time, sunrise might become your favorite part of the day. The convenient thing about the latitude of the tropics is that the sun waits a little longer to rise, so you don't have to wake up before six to catch it. I'll admit that I only witness one or two sunrises a week, but they're pretty amazing if you're blessed with a clear day on the ocean's horizon. Another pleasant aspect of morning is that the temperature is comfortably cool. There's an aesthetic quality to walking around the empty pool. Also, the beach is a beautiful place to sip a cup of coffee while the rows of chairs are vacant.

Can we reserve our seats?

Every resort has a policy on saving seats, but few ever enforce it. During the busier seasons, chairs along the pool and beach will be claimed around mid-morning. By lunchtime it can be difficult to find a spot. Most resorts have a sign stating that after a half-hour, the reserved seats can be cleared off, although this doesn't seem to ever happen. A lot of people get up around sunrise to "call dibs" on chairs. Usually they'll put towels and a few possessions on their pair of seats—maybe a book or an old t-shirt—to stake a claim. 99% of the guests are okay with this and understand that the seat claimers will eventually make their way out shortly after breakfast. We've only seen one occasion where some old folks argued about their territory.

If you're at a busier value resort, attempting to reserve seats could get ugly. There are online videos of people arguing about the rules. If contacted, management has to enforce their half-hour policy. It's rare, because normally people are mature enough to not cause problems, but if you're attempting to save a prime spot, know there's a potential for conflict.

My wife and I are early birds, so we're normally at our spot by 8:30 in the morning. We don't have to fret about policy. If you want a seat located in what you think is a prime position, show up early and be prepared to protect it.

Choosing the right spot

The morning is often a time to recover from the previous night's debauchery. It might seem like a good idea to claim chairs right next to the bar, but you're going to be around a lot of foot traffic. We prefer the beach chairs in the morning. While reading a book, there is no better background noise than waves crashing. And while some resorts have Wi-Fi on parts of their beach, sitting there is usually an effective way to force yourself to disconnect.

If you arrive early enough, you can claim a front row spot so that you can look straight out into the ocean. A word of caution, though—sometimes you'll end up next to loud talkers. Avoid the spots with more than two seats claimed, because you're going to encounter a talkative group rehashing the previous evening. If it's going to bother you, avoid smokers and people who bring their own speakers as well. Not everyone is considerate.

No matter where you decide to set up camp, make sure there's an umbrella. Most resorts cover a majority of their seats with some shade. While it's safe to lie out in the sun earlier in the morning, it's going to roast you later on. You may have to adjust your seats as the shadows shift, but it's better than sunburn.

What should we know about the beach?

Depending on the beach, the Atlantic coastlines are calmer than the Pacific. If you have children, do not let them swim in the ocean unsupervised. There are usually lifeguards, but they accept no liability for your safety. Stay within the ropes of your resort.

There will be flags lining the beach telling you of the water conditions. I've never seen a green flag suggesting that the water is calm. They're always at least yellow, representing caution. On most days the flags are red signaling dangerous conditions, but you're still allowed to swim. Use common sense and good judgment when entering the water. Blue flags caution you about incoming jellyfish, so stay out of the water when you see any blue flags.

The seaweed situation in the Cancun/Riviera Maya region has unfortunately become worse over the years. It depends on the time of year and the weather. Some days, you might be blessed with clear water, and other times the ocean might be plagued with so much seaweed that you can't enjoy a swim. Some resorts have a tractor with an attachment that cleans the beach up. Others have men raking the debris. It's frustrating, but there isn't much you can do about it. The Dominican Republic is home to nicer beaches with less seaweed and clearer water. And while the water in the Pacific isn't as clear, it doesn't have as much seaweed.

Sometimes there are fish, but they're harmless. Look out for rocks before you go frolicking in the waves. Usually the ocean floor is smooth, but be careful your first time out. Do not swim if there are large rocks near the shore. The waves are powerful enough to knock you into them.

Many beaches are habitats for sea turtles. These are endangered, so resorts will go out of their way to protect them. If you see a nest (a small pile of sand usually surrounded by a small cage), do not tamper with it. Tampering is a criminal offense and carries an extreme penalty. At one resort, they actually closed the beach at 9:00 due to nightly sea turtle activity. If you have aspirations to be on the beach late at night, talk to the resort about this possibility ahead of time.

Some resorts will host activities where you can witness baby sea turtles hatching; we were lucky enough to see this in Costa Rica. Again, do not take it upon yourself to interact with the sea turtles.

When you return from the beach to the pool area, always shower off. There are multiple showers to rinse your feet or entire body, so that you don't track sand into the pool. Parents, please make sure your children get in this habit too.

Are there topless women on the beach?

During our honeymoon in the Dominican Republic, I suspected my wife had set up a test. There were nearly a half-dozen topless women sunbathing on any given day. In other cultures, it's not as big of a deal as it is in the U.S. The Mexican beaches normally have less of this than other countries around the Caribbean, and if it's a family resort, they ask that women refrain from topless sunbathing. Europeans have different social norms, so it's important not to stare or think too ethnocentrically.

Check the online reviews, because there are certain resorts aimed more for singles where clothing is optional on the beach, but those are adults-only. There's even a resort in Jamaica that has its own little island that basically serves as its own nudist colony. This resort isn't on our places-to-visit list.

Is there anything else we should know about the beach?

Vendors are the most annoying part of being on the beach. Throughout the day, they'll walk up and down carrying cheap souvenirs and calling for your attention. A dismissive nod normally does the trick to get rid of them. I say, "Don't feed the bears"—you should discourage these vendors so that everyone can enjoy a more relaxed beach experience—but other people insist on giving them business, even though the items are low-quality and probably made in China.

Chapter 7
Services and Meals

Whom should we tip?

For every trip, my wife and I bring along a stack of one-dollar bills and a smaller stack of fives. You're not required to tip anyone, but common courtesy implies that you should, especially the workers delivering something to your room.

The first person you'll tip is the shuttle driver from the airport to the resort. Your vacation guide will mention this as you arrive. The driver is usually the one who loads and unloads your luggage, so give him a few bucks.

The bellhop is the next person to take care of. Always use the bellhop just to make sure you're going the right way. He gets at least a five. We got ours a shot of tequila once, but he declined.

I tip bartenders, but not on every drink. I wish I could, but I would run out of money. Plus, no one likes to carry around a pocket of soggy bills through the pool. I normally tip the swim-up bartender on my first drink of the day and periodically throughout. If they were extraordinary, I shell out extra at the end of the week.

The bartenders at the various resort bars should be tipped as well, especially for more specialized drinks. Some of them work hours before it gets busy, so help them out as they provide cocktails you normally wouldn't order.

We tip our housekeeper every day. This usually results in special treatment, such as towels folded into swans or decorations of some sort. Occasionally we'll get a complimentary tray of fruit or cake with a bottle of champagne for being repeat guests. Tip your turndown service too. They'll leave you decorations and desserts if you do.

If you order room service, have the courtesy to tip generously. These workers have to cart food around many miles a day in the hot weather, so they definitely earn it. As soon as you order, have the money ready by the door.

Sometimes resorts have food carts around the pool. I turn into a child when a random ice cream cart pulls up. The last resort we visited had crepe carts. Give these folks a tip for the bonus service they provide while they stand out in the sun.

Even though breakfast and lunch are usually buffet style, you'll still have servers bringing you drinks and clearing plates from your table. Even a modest tip is appreciated. Oddly enough, dinner service isn't always great, no matter which resort you're at. Tip accordingly.

Don't ask ignorant questions

Though your curious mind might be innocent, try to refrain from asking the staff members questions about how rough their lives are. Inevitably, we'll hear someone suggest that a worker should visit whatever city they're from in the United States. People also ask workers about the number of hours they have to work, wages, and even more personal and uncomfortable topics. It's none of your business. Just tip well.

Advice on Meals

If drinking too much doesn't upset your system, overeating can. I've learned the hard way not to stuff my face right away, especially after dieting for ten weeks. I've only suffered from food-poisoning once (seafood ceviche in the Dominican Republic at a so-so resort), but there have been plenty of times where my appetite abandoned me mid-week.

Avoid red meat at the buffets. Once I started doing this, I had fewer problems. Find something grilled fresh at lunch. Bacon for breakfast should be eaten in moderation. I believe what throws my stomach into knots the most is the excess desserts. They're abundant at the buffets, and when you combine that much sugar with alcohol, you're inviting stomach woes.

Breakfast

Even before the breakfast buffet opens, coffee will be available. Either the resort will have a coffee cafe or you can find some in front of the main dining area. And of course, every room should have a coffee maker of its own (but who wants to do that?).

Most resorts rely on a buffet for breakfast, but some offer an additional a la carte option (or free room service at finer resorts). Because the buffet has the largest selection and we want a good spot on the beach, we always go there for breakfast. Just as with desserts, watch how much sugar you take in. You don't want to crash mid-morning.

Occasionally I'll have a mimosa or ask for a shot of Bailey's for my coffee. I don't drink Bloody Marys, but if you do, know there isn't any judgment on vacation. And don't worry, most places serve breakfast from 7 to 11:00, so sleep in as needed. It's not required to dress up for breakfast, although men are still forbidden to wear sleeveless shirts.

Lunch

Lunch brings options. I'll admit to usually having a drink or five before lunchtime. I've been in the water quite a bit too, so it's unpleasant to march back to the place breakfast was served to sit in the air conditioning while still dripping. If that sounds like an inconvenience, a popular resort option is grilled food near the pool area. An outdoor buffet is a quick and easy option without losing your spot or troubling with a t-shirt. Hop in line, and you're eating moments later.

If you're going back inside to eat, towel off and clothe yourself first. Most respectable resorts will make sure everyone is wearing a cover-up or shirt instead of swimwear for lunch. We saw a woman in a bikini removed from the dining area because she failed to wear a cover-up. Along with common courtesy, it keeps the resort in compliance with the health code.

A la carte restaurants are often attached to the grilling station. While it's great to taste foreign and exotic foods, lunch is usually good ol' American items like burgers and buffalo wings with French fries. Healthier options are available back where you had breakfast, but we prefer to stay outside mid-day.

Lunch is a convenient time to let your liver catch its breath if you hit the bar earlier. I attempt to gulp down as much water as possible while trying not to take in all carbs. The afternoon crash is sometimes inevitable, but there are ways to delay it.

Over the many trips, I've found quite a range of ice cream quality. Some resorts have the messy but incredibly fun soft-serve machines. Typically, the ice cream is scoop-it-yourself and cross your fingers on the quality. I hadn't had much luck until this most recent vacation, when I discovered the best banana ice cream I've ever tasted. It was a challenge to limit my lactose intake.

If you eat outside, keep an eye on your plate, because the birds will swoop in and steal anything from it. If you don't see a busboy, at least cover your scraps with a napkin when you leave.

Eating in the pool is forbidden. No one wants to come into contact with a soggy nacho.

Dinner

Going to a fancy dinner every night is my wife's favorite part of vacation. It's like going out on a date, eating and drinking all you want, and then not having to worry about paying or driving home. If your relationship lacks date nights, this is a perfect opportunity to catch up. We've even begun a tradition of having me "pick her up" from the room to simulate that early stage of our relationship.

The average resort will have four to six different dinner options to choose from. If you insist on buffets, the resort always has one open. If you're dining with children, this is probably the best option, as the other places require a bit of patience (and they don't have menus to color on).

At least once a week, resorts will hold an outdoor dinner-fiesta buffet. These are usually followed by a show later on in the evening. If you buy a bottle of wine, you get the best seats up front. These can be a lot of fun because the air tends to cool once the sun goes down. You sit at a large table with other guests and chat about vacation experiences.

A photographer will make his or her way around and take couples' pictures that they paste onto souvenir bottles, onto shot glasses, or into festive frames. They're an inexpensive token to take home.

Onto the restaurants. The most common restaurant types are Italian, Mexican, seafood, steakhouse, and Japanese (sushi with the choice of a hibachi grill). We've also encountered Mediterranean and French at our favorite resorts.

At the finer resorts, you don't need to make a reservation, with one exception—if you're planning on eating at the hibachi grill. In my opinion, hibachi grills are like piano bars. They're fun while you're in your twenties with a large group, but once you reach an age where you feel like you've experienced them enough, the thrill is gone.

You should take into account that you're not at an American restaurant. Dining in a different country is something you need to adjust to while abroad. For example, instead of a professional server who knows how to match wines with even the most exotic of entrees, you'll experience servers who often haven't mastered English just yet. They're plenty competent at the basics, but the dinner serving position is apparently not a senior one. Therefore, exercise your patience and don't expect long explanations about the foods. Often times these servers fill other roles on the resort as well. They sometimes serve in more than one restaurant, too.

Another key difference is the pace at which dinner is served. There have been evenings when we arrived early and our dinner was served quickly, but that isn't always the case. Still, what's the rush? We're quite content even when it takes a little longer than usual. The rest of the world is okay with this slower pace, so relax your American mental timer and enjoy the bottomless cocktails.

Once you are seated, you'll notice an unnecessary amount of plating and glassware. They'll give you a menu along with a wine list. You can order house wine for no extra charge, but everything on the wine menu is an extra cost (so we always decline it).

Ordinarily, the menu is divided into Spanish and English. Other than that fact, the fancy naming, and the fact that prices aren't listed, it's not that different from a menu back at home: appetizers, salads, soups, pastas, entrees and desserts. Just like on a cruise, you should be able to get as many as you want when you're at a finer resort. The appetizers and salads are much smaller portions than you're used to, but they are beautifully plated, which you can appreciate.

No matter which restaurant you're at, they often have the same basic entree options: pasta, beef/steak, chicken, fish (usually salmon or sea bass), and then something slightly different like veal, duck, or a vegetarian option. You don't need to fret about the fancy pronunciation, because the server just needs to know the basic entree you want.

Sometimes dinner includes live music. Instead of bands, a couple mariachis might sing near your table. My wife is an expert at gaining their interest (tip them if they sing to your table). Other times you may get a violinist or a guitarist. Enjoy the cultural differences and take your time eating.

We usually have a lot of fun exercising our minimal Spanish skills with the servers. They're charming, and if they're aware of committing a mistake, they'll do everything they can to make up for it. It's no surprise that restaurants with an open bar policy are happier places.

Save room for dessert. They aren't large, but they're wonderfully plated. My wife never wants dessert, so I often make the mistake of indulging in two orders.

What is the romantic dinner package?

This has been offered at every resort we've visited. It's always $200, so we've never splurged. Basically, you and your partner will eat a special private dinner along the beach. There are usually no more than half a dozen couples per night, if that. The menu is different, usually offering lobster as a main entree, and you might be required to order a special bottle of wine at some venues. If you're going to propose, this would be the most romantic time to pull it off. The decor and setting is very elegant, so if you can afford it, I'm sure it leaves a lasting memory.

Late-night eats

The dinner buffet might stay open until 11:00 at some resorts. If not, one of the bars will have snacks in it, although the best option is room service if your resort provides it. You can kiss your in-shape body goodbye as you indulge in greasy food and live like royalty!

What is a privacy door?

Privacy doors are rare, but one of the most convenient amenities in a resort. A privacy door is a latched door between the hallway and a shelf in one of your closets. When you're expecting room service, you unlatch the privacy door so that the food can be dropped off without the delivery man ever entering your room. Leave your tip money there and avoid having to make yourself presentable every time you order room service. When you finish eating, you can stack the empty plates back on that shelf in the closet. Without a privacy door, the server has to enter your room to deliver everything, which may infringe upon your late-night activities. Hurray for privacy doors!

Summing up the food situation...

Resort food may not be as outstanding as food on a cruise, but we enjoy almost all of our meals. Understand that they cannot always provide the finest steaks at an all-inclusive resort. The more expensive resorts will obviously have higher quality food. Either way, the flavoring will be different than what you and your stomach are used to, especially if you diet for weeks ahead of time. And while you want to get the most for your money, be careful of overindulging, especially on the sweeter items. Your system is already handling an excess of alcohol, so try and take it easy every few meals. My advice is to taper back on breakfast and lunch, even though they're buffets, and then enjoy a full dinner.

Chapter 8
Staying Active

What's a typical day of resort life?

Unless you're an energetic twenty-something, understand that you can't "steal time." If you wake up early and party early, it's going to catch up with you by mid-afternoon. If you stay up until the bars close, you're going to miss the beauty of the morning. Over the years, my wife and I have shifted into being the early birds of the resort. We've also discovered the benefit of taking naps.

On an ideal morning, we wake a little after 7 o'clock. If we crashed early the night before, either of us could be up and at the gym around 6:30. We get to breakfast at 7:30 and are back at the room packing for the beach around 8. My wife likes to read and snooze a little more while I play around in the ocean or walk back up for another coffee.

Around 10:00, the morning and sunlight shifts as the pool starts to populate and the swim-up bar opens. I'll admit, most days I start drinking right around this time. A good buzz leads into lunch around 12:30. In the afternoon as the beach livens up, we venture over to the pool to frequent the swim-up bar. We swim while people watching and chat until around 3 or 4 in the afternoon. During this time, housekeeping always takes care of our room.

The late-afternoon nap has become a staple. It feels amazing to come back to an air-conditioned, freshly cleaned room for a pre-nap shower. If you're tipsy, be careful on the granite floors. Ideally we wake up from our slumber around 5:30, but there have been times when a few extra hours just happened. There was one occasion where we didn't wake up until 1:00 a.m., and by that point we'd missed the whole evening. This is what I mean about not stealing time. If you hit the day too hard, you miss out on the night.

Typically, my wife needs around an hour to get ready. By 6:00 I'm cleaned up, so I get dressed and head to the martini bar near the lobby or the sports bar to catch up on the scores from home. I have my own tradition of ordering an old-fashioned and chatting up a sports fan if there's one nearby. My wife will text me when she's ready, so I walk back to the room to "pick her up" and escort her to wherever we're eating. This is when we call for turndown service and anything else our room might need such as more bottles of water. The walk to dinner is a great time for pictures, because there should be just enough sunlight and we're already dressed up.

The restaurants normally open at 6:30, so we never have to wait for a seat. Dinner should take around 90 minutes depending on how busy they are and whether you get dessert. After our meal, we normally find a table at one of the bars and get a few more drinks. My wife and I always bring a pack of cards to play, but after a few hands we end up talking until we've hit our limits. Bars often have some low-key live music like a pianist or lounge singer.

If it's been a longer evening, we'll order room service, hydrate, take some aspirin and call it a night so that we're ready to do it all over the next day.

Do people have sex on the beach?

Every couple tries it once. And once only.

What are some tips to feel normal?

Depending on your lifestyle and habits back at home, a vacation can wear your body out. Remember, you're not in your usual environment, and the climate alone can lead to discomfort if you're not careful. Make sure you're limiting your time in the sun. Try to get as much sleep as you need, and in extreme cases, you can even take a day off from drinking.

Hydrate throughout the day even when you don't feel thirsty. Along with walking around the resort, get at least a little bit of exercise through daily activities. I admit that I feel much better when I wake up early enough to squeeze in a workout.

Don't forget to eat the occasional vegetable at lunch and dinner. There's a lot of sugary options, but your body still needs nutrition to hold up throughout the week. Skip dessert if you're full, and limit the spicy food, especially at night.

Take care of your feet. You'll be walking around barefoot or in flip-flops a majority of the time, so mind your paws. It's not uncommon to stub a toe, so pay attention when you're intoxicated.

And naps. Take 'em!

What are the usual activities around the resort?

It's tempting to spend the whole day drinking and snoozing, but at least a few times during your week you should try participating in one of the resort's daily activities. These are posted around the property, and the finer resorts will deliver them on a daily update sheet during turn-down service.

Some resorts may have one-of-a-kind activities that you can only find at that particular place. For example, one of the resorts we visit organizes a one-mile hike down the beach to a lagoon. Be sure to check the daily schedule and plan the activities you don't want to miss around your drinking.

Yoga/Pilates/Fitness

Basic fitness classes begin between 7 and 9 in the morning. There's either a small pavilion or a location on the beach. Beach yoga tends to be more popular as it allows for a multi-purpose social media picture. Don't worry about classes being too advanced. The instructors are laid back and will adapt to your level. If it's a slower week, you might get one-on-one instruction. These classes are a safer option than working out on your own if you're just getting back into exercising.

Biking

Some resorts own a few bicycles where you can pedal around with a small group. I'll refrain from over-explaining this.

Ping-pong

I don't know how anyone plays this outside in such a breezy area, but occasionally they put the table in a game room.

Billiards

The cues aren't always great, but neither is my ability. We squeeze in a game or two before lunch sometimes. There should be a game room with a functioning pool table.

Archery/Air Rifles

They usually set up a competition for whoever participates. Like billiards, don't expect the best equipment, but it's fun. These are usually held mid-morning before the average guest begins drinking.

Water aerobics

This activity is a staple around noon at every resort. The busiest part of the pool is taken over with around two dozen participants every day. One of the entertainment staff members will lead the group through what appear to be not-so-strenuous exercises.

We've also visited resorts with underwater spin bikes which are a more challenging activity. Last summer my wife tried an aerobics class called Aquaforce where everyone balanced on small floating mattresses. Even though these classes are often populated by women, men are welcome to take part.

Various sports

There are a handful of small competitions adapted for the pool. Volleyball is a popular activity (available on the beach as well). There are also competitions setup for shooting, throwing, or tossing something through a target. Look for bocce ball, shuffleboard, or giant checkers/chess around the pool area too. On our honeymoon I ended up playing goalie in a water polo game. My wife fed me shots throughout the competition.

Kayaking

Kayaking in the ocean is so much better than drifting down a scummy river in the Midwest. You're allowed to paddle your kayak well into the sea, and since it's a free activity, they don't care how long you're out there. I highly recommend trying this, so you can experience the solitude of the ocean beyond the buoys.

Sailing

Every trip, I say I'm going to learn how to sail, and every trip I chicken out. At some resorts the lesson is free, but since it's in the late afternoon, it's easy to overlook it. The boats are small and basic, but they expect you to know what you're doing if you take one out.

Crazy Games

Crazy games are held in the pool later in the afternoon, because the participants are normally drunk. These involve relay races against the staff and other silly competitions where people let themselves go.

Classes

Turns out education can be fun. Spanish, cooking, salsa dancing and other classes are common half-hour sessions at most resorts. My favorite is tequila tasting. You'll be surprised at some of the fine liquors they'll share to educate you.

Bingo

Usually held at the swim-up bar, bingo is another game meant to appeal to the intoxicated. The boards are waterproof, and along with learning numbers in different languages, you might win some prizes.

Casino

We've been to resorts where they bring the (waterproof) casino games into the pool. Ever play blackjack on a raft? You can! There's no actual gambling involved, but they give you chips to simulate it. You might find a casino night setup after dinner at least once a week if you're keen on fake gambling.

Market night

Most resorts allow local merchants to set up souvenir stands in the main plaza several nights a week. You'll get a better selection and price than the resort's gift shop, but be careful what you purchase. The items aren't as authentic as they appear. This is your chance to haggle and bargain your way to a deal. It's part of the culture. We've purchased a handful of (most likely unlicensed) sports merchandise. For example, you can always find painted skulls wearing helmets of all 32 NFL teams. These were listed at $50, but I haggled my way down to $20. My strategy is to show the vendor that I only brought so much cash down from the room, that way they know if they can't meet my price, I'm walking away. It's really fun once you get the hang of it, and don't worry, they're still making a solid profit.

At one resort they had an art dealer who was trying to sell paintings for thousands of dollars. Before you buy anything of value, ask yourself how secure your merchandise will be on the flight home.

Vacation bingo

Vacation bingo is a tradition my wife and I started a few years ago. We noticed that we see a lot of the same types of people on every trip. Most of them are committing mild faux pas—for example, the man taking a picture of the food at the buffet or the dude running down the beach filming himself with a selfie stick. I won't pretend all of our bingo squares are politically correct, but if you and your partner have inside jokes and a little experience in people watching, you can make your own bingo boards and play throughout the week.

You can also add challenges to your bingo game. For example, the first one to participate in a resort activity; first one to hit the gym; first one to do a shot (my favorite). One year after our bus dropped us off, we were waiting in line to check in. I told my wife I needed to use the restroom, but instead, I snuck over to the bar and ordered two shots of tequila. I took my shot, brought her the other, and checked off the first square on my board.

What is the evening entertainment like?

I can sum it up best by saying you shouldn't expect Broadway. These are young entertainers who are working their way up the showbiz ladder, and while their abs will put anyone's to shame, the shows are hit or miss.

The performers are very talented in what they do. If you like choreographed dance, you'll enjoy the show. It's when they try to do too much that the productions seem to fall short.

The shows typically start at 9 pm in a theater that sits a few hundred. Drinking will definitely enhance the experience. You may notice the show is hosted by the same staff member who led water aerobics, so imagine how long of a day it's been for that person.

What types of shows are there?

The one we notice most resorts putting on is the Michael Jackson tribute show. It's an hour of lip syncing and dancing to your favorite MJ hits.

Best of Broadway is another greatest hits dancing production. You might get other international flavors of dance and costumes depending on the theme.

As a stand-up comedian myself (translation: comedy snob), I always skip the comedian they book. The acts are usually hacky, but your tastes may vary. Along with comedians, you might see hypnotists and magicians too. Again, these are up to your tastes and by that point in the evening, it may not take much to entertain you. At a family resort, expect extra hackiness.

On some nights, you might be treated to live music. This normally happens out in the plaza near one of the bars slightly earlier in the evening. Expect to hear covers with a foreign flavor. I always enjoy when they play a classic song from a different culture, because it's interesting to hear other people sing along to their country's well-known tunes that most of us Americans have never heard.

Are there nightclubs?

Most resorts offer a bar with a DJ for dancing late into the night. We've met a lot of guests who venture out in cabs to the more urban areas to experience the nightlife. I cannot recommend this. In my opinion, there's no need to leave the open bars of your resort and risk struggling to find a way back in the middle of the night. I've also been warned that men are very aggressive at these clubs, no matter who you are.

Alone time

As the week goes on, you'll fall into a bit of a routine. You might discover a favorite spot by the pool or a restaurant that stands out from the others. A week is a long time to spend every moment together, even if it's your honeymoon, so don't forget to make a little time for yourself. Take short walks around the resort or down the beach while your partner naps, just to give each other a break. My wife was adamant that I include this advice! You can try the resort activities by yourself, and no one will think less of you.

Chapter 9
Day Trips

What are day trips like and how do we book them?

Day trips are potentially the most memorable moments of your vacation. You have the ability to visit places unlike anything else in your motherland. These trips include plenty of options and can take anywhere from a few hours to a full day. My wife and I have experienced a variety of adventures, and have even discovered a few worth repeating. Be sure they're in your budget, because you don't want to miss this opportunity.

Is it better to book ahead of time?

A reputable vacation company will be stationed at your hotel if you prefer the safest option. Normally, they start plugging the day trips on the shuttle ride to the resort. You can wait until you're there to book, but it might cost a little more. By booking it this way, they get their cut of a marked-up price. However, a few years ago my wife and I started booking our trips ahead of time, and it's always worked better for us.

Find a website (like Travelocity) with a suitable number of reviews for the trips. Once you find an adventure you're interested in, do a full investigation on all it entails. Make sure you're physically fit enough to hike in the heat if it's part of the trip. Or if your swimming skills are limited and you get seasick easily, you'll want to find a trip that stays on land.

Another advantage to booking ahead of time is making sure there's availability. Some of the more popular trips might only be available on certain days, so it's best to double-check and reserve your spot three to four weeks out. Many of them require no payment until the actual day of the trip. They'll contact you about which resort you're staying at and then arrange for your pickup that morning. You need to notify them via email of your room number; they'll need that to enter the resort on the morning they pick you up.

We've also noticed that pre-booked day trips have fewer people. Unless you splurge on a private tour, your shuttle to your day trip will probably stop at other resorts. This is time-consuming, especially when you're first to be picked up and last to be dropped off. If you're at the resort with a larger group, you might be lucky enough to fill the whole trip with your group and avoid having to add strangers.

What should we know about all day trips?

Be sure to get a good night's sleep. This isn't something you want to experience with a hangover, so take it easy the night before so you're prepared for a long but exciting day.

The shuttle ride to and from your destination is the worst part. Depending on logistics, they might pick you up before your resort even opens for breakfast, so figure out how you can eat ahead of time. These trips almost always include lunch, but that won't be for hours. Swipe some fruit at the buffet the day before to take with you.

You'll be on your trip with people from other countries who speak other languages. Your guide will be multilingual, but he or she will communicate everything in at least Spanish and English. Spending a day with someone from a different culture is usually a great experience, but we have had some issues.

For example, Italians have a different idea than Americans as to what makes a comfortable temperature. On one particular trip which involved an hour of riding in the back of a van, we started to overheat. My wife reached up and opened the vents so that the air conditioning could cool us off. It wasn't strong, but it was enough to make conditions tolerable.

A family of Italians with two girls sat in the row ahead of us. Within moments, they became cold and reached up to close the vents. (The look on my wife's face!) My wife opened them back up, and they must have understood enough English to interpret, "I'm about to puke on you!" We've shared this anecdote with enough travelers to confirm that yes, Italians prefer a disgustingly warm temperature in their vehicles.

You might also encounter cultures who are a little freer with their bodies. They aren't as shy about nudity. Don't stare, just accept that standards are different around the world. If you're bringing your kids, explain this thoroughly.

If a trip says it's going to take all day, it will. Don't count on getting back to the pool by mid-afternoon. Other cultures are not as hurried as America, so they take their time on just about everything. See it as a day to detox and make memories. This is particularly apparent when it comes time to eat. A lunch that takes most Americans fifteen minutes to consume, other cultures will spread out over an hour. Enjoy the scenery when you've finished eating, and snap some photos.

There may be additional stops along your trip. Think of these as a bonus instead of obstacles. For example, your shuttle might stop at a gift shop for a restroom break and encourage you to support the local economy if you use the facility. One year in the Dominican Republic our truck stopped by a guy named "The Snake Man." We all took turns as he draped his harmless snakes around our shoulders for a picture. We each gave him a few bucks and everyone was happier.

A lot of these trips offer alcohol on the way, especially if you're riding in a boat, so make sure you can handle traveling while intoxicated. You may also want to plan out the restroom situation.

Speaking of that, the restrooms you'll visit on a day trip are third-world sanitation. Don't expect indoor plumbing and running water. A lot of times they request that the toilet paper be disposed of in the trash instead of the toilet (which is a hole in the ground). There will be means to wash your hands, but the toilets you'll encounter won't soon be forgotten.

If you get carsick easily, ask to sit up front. You might spend hours on roads that aren't paved to the standards you're used to. It's a bumpy ride into the wilderness, and we've ridden with many people who have puked on the way to or from the destination. Even if you don't get carsick, motion sickness pills are a great idea.

The person managing your tour values his or her job highly, so if you need help with anything, they're very understanding and patient people. However, don't use this as an excuse to be a high-maintenance jerk. These people often work 12-hour shifts for weeks in a row without a day off.

One of the most memorable guides we've ever had was a man named Sammy. He took us around the Dominican Republic in a large truck where we all sat in the back. While flying down the highway, he hung off the back tailgate mixing drinks with one hand and holding on with the other. He was incredibly friendly and energetic, so we tipped him very generously.

You should always tip your guide at the end of the tour. This should be one of the largest tips you shell out during your vacation. Whatever these guides make from their company, assume that it's not fair compensation for what they put up with on a daily basis.

How do we photograph our day trip?

Taking a cellphone along can be risky depending on the activity, so there's always waterproof options like GoPro. The more adventurous trips will include a photographer who captures great pictures and video of you and your group from difficult angles. At the end of the day, they'll offer you a photo package of your adventure. These range from $30 to $60, but we've never been disappointed in our investment. You'll receive the footage via email that week.

What should we pack for day trips?

When you book your trip, you should receive a specific list of items to pack in your beach bag or backpack. You might need to bring towels from the resort (which they may require you to sign out). Depending on if there's water or not, a spare change of clothes and aqua socks can help. Pack some bug spray unless you're told not to bring any. If you're swimming in a freshwater river or lake, they won't want it polluted with the toxic chemicals from bug spray. They may even have you rinse off your sunblock too. Fear not—If this is the situation, they will provide sunblock and bug spray that is nature-friendly after you dry off.

Bring cash to tip and purchase souvenirs. A five-dollar bill is powerful in a gift shop in the middle of nowhere. It's safe to leave your possessions locked in the van. I've never heard of anything being stolen because no one wants to harm the tourist industry. The locations you travel to are remote enough that no criminals are wandering around, breaking into vehicles.

What's the day trip lunch like?

When lunch is included on your trip, you can expect the local cuisine: beans and rice. Sometimes you might get fish or a more conventional sandwich if the guide packs the lunches. For the more popular spots, it's picnic buffet style. You'll gather in a pavilion and taste the organic version of whatever they're serving. You might get to try foods you wouldn't find at the resort or back at home. Turns out I enjoy cactus.

Ziplining and rappelling

On our honeymoon, which was our first trip together, we agreed that ziplining was definitely the first activity we wanted to try. It's just thrilling enough to muster a little adrenaline, but unless you're crossing a large canyon, it's not pee-your-pants terrifying. The ziplines varied in length from around 50 to 300 yards, and we felt safe the entire time. The forests you'll zipline through usually include a little hiking, but it's a great experience. Read the reviews to see how extreme the ziplines are.

Rappelling takes a little more physical ability. It can feel dangerous scaling down a cliff, but it doesn't take long to get the hang of it. One trip allowed us to rappel down a cliff right next to a waterfall. Instruction and equipment is top-notch, so if you can conquer your fear of heights, it's an enriching, memorable experience.

Plantation visits

Some trips include a trip to a chocolate or coffee plantation. This visit might be combined with something like ziplining to fill the day with a variety of activities. If you're into something more low-key with some culture, it's a favorable option. We've only visited one during our honeymoon at Punta Cana in the Dominican Republic.

A word of caution: They will try to sell you whatever goods the plantation produces. For example, we tasted the best coffee and hot chocolate from their sample and then bought $20 worth to bring home. Somehow our batch wasn't nearly as tasty.

Canyoning

Canyoning is an advanced version of hiking, so unless you have at least intermediate agility, you should pass. We hiked through the rocks along a river, crossing it several times along the way. Aqua socks were a must because of necessary traction for safety. On the way back, we floated through parts of the river and even got to jump off a few cliffs. Use your discretion when booking this kind of adventure.

Tequila factory/tasting

The tequila factory was a bonus stop on the way back from a ziplining trip. It included six free samples, so we definitely supported the local economy by purchasing a bottle. I can still recall the smell of the agave they roasted in front of us.

Another trip we discovered in the Cancun area was a private tequila tasting at a rooftop pool. These small businesses pop up, so you may need to provide your own transportation. If you're within 15 minutes, the cab fares are reasonable. These independent trips will need to be booked ahead of time. I suggest paying with PayPal so you have consumer protection.

Catamaran boat trip

These trips can be rather pleasant and relaxing, provided the sea isn't choppy that day. A van shuttles you to a dock where you'll load a boat. The staff is always upbeat and energetic, so enjoy their efforts. Drinks are provided throughout the day, and you'll receive lunch at the turnaround point.

In the Caribbean, you'll experience the bluest of water. The Pacific isn't as beautiful, but compensates with a better look at marine life. Either way, you'll boat for a couple hours until you get to a beach where they'll feed you and let you swim or snorkel for an hour or so. Sometimes there are other boats there, but they won't infringe on your area.

Catamaran tours are some of the most affordable trips. As a bonus, you might encounter the ocean's wildlife on your way home while the sun sets. In Costa Rica we were treated to rays and dolphins leaping from the water just behind our boat. We've also encountered sea turtles and even the occasional whale. The possibilities make the trip back to the dock more enjoyable.

Sunset cruises and "booze cruises"

These are heavily marketed in the airport, but my wife and I haven't seen the point in paying extra for meals and drinks. To be honest, by sunset we're already boozed up. Plus, a booze cruise is aimed more for the singles, so if you're vacationing stag, it would be a better investment. If you need a romantic dinner for two, try the sunset dinner cruises. Check the reviews and find one worth the cost. The sun sets much earlier in the tropics, so they may not keep you out incredibly late.

Deep-sea fishing

We've never tried this, but if you take your fishing seriously, these trips are a must. I can't imagine the cost of transporting whatever you catch back with you and having it mounted. However, if you're just in it to catch and release a creature you'd never encounter in the water at home, give it a shot. There are certain resorts where you can arrange to have them prep and cook your catch for you, but again, there's going to be a considerable fee.

Parasailing

Parasailing is something you can book on your resort's beach. The advantage is that you won't have to travel anywhere, you just book a time. I've tried it once, and though it's a beautiful view, there wasn't much of a thrill or rush. However, if the price is right and you want a quick ride and some fantastic photo opportunities, it's available.

Swim and snorkel with the...

Dolphins

This is popular, but we feel too sorry for the captive dolphins, so we haven't tried it. They're in the ocean, but dividers keep them from swimming away. Additionally, it's family-friendly, so expect a higher percentage of children on this one.

Starfish

We tried this once in the Dominican Republic. Snorkeling is fun, but the only two starfish magically appeared in the hands of our guide. It's basic snorkeling with a catamaran ride.

Turtles

This was excellent! Numerous sea turtles floated by as we swam around them. The staff remind you not to touch any of the wildlife for obvious reasons.

Whale sharks

Though pricey, this was one of the most amazing experiences we've had on vacation. After an hour of bouncing over the waves, our boat was one of many to circle around the area where the Earth's sixth largest creatures hang out. They're humongous, but mellow. A small amount of swimming and snorkeling ability means you'll have a better experience, but isn't strictly necessary. You get several chances to swim alongside these giants for a short interval. We captured some amazing up-close videos, too.

Mayan ruins

If you're traveling to the very popular Cancun region of Mexico, you have the opportunity to visit ancient Mayan pyramids and other ruins. My wife and I had the pleasure of scaling the tallest pyramid in the region. Getting up wasn't that challenging; however, the climb down took a lot of concentration. I've heard there is the occasional nasty accident, but if you're in decent shape and coordinated enough, you shouldn't have any trouble.

If you definitely want to climb a pyramid, check ahead of time to see if it's still allowed. Chichén Itzá, one of the Seven Wonders of the World, has not been climbable since 2003. Coba is a better bet. It was just the right amount of challenge for us.

Along with visiting the incredible sights, you'll be educated by your guide who will fascinate you with facts about the Mayan culture. We even received an authentic Mayan blessing at the end of our tour. It was the summer of 2012, so they also explained to us that the Mayans did not predict the world was coming to an end that December. Their simple explanation was that their calendar was merely resetting.

A word of caution—any time you're visiting a historic sight, it's going to be a long drive from your resort. The highways aren't nearly as smooth or fast as you're used to, so expect a long, fairly uncomfortable ride both ways.

Exploring cenotes

A cenote is a natural sinkhole where a cave ceiling has collapsed. These beautiful and hidden pools of water were sacred to the Mayans because they provided them with fresh water. You can now take a day trip to these fascinating sights and swim around the caves. You'll definitely have to rinse any bug spray or sunscreen off before entering, but it's worth it.

Mud baths and hot springs

One year in Costa Rica we took a trip with a plethora of activities. First, we encountered a place where mud bubbled from a spout in the earth. We coated our skin with the gray mud and let it dry. (Fortunately, we were the first ones through, because some nearby monkeys began throwing feces from the trees at the people just behind us!)

After rinsing off as best we could, we were shown a choice of natural pools where water temperatures ranged from chilled to way-too-hot. After finding a comfortable pool, we relaxed in the jungle and listened to the wildlife (especially the aforementioned monkeys).

This trip also included a man-made water slide that stretched a quarter of a mile down a hillside. It was quite the bonus to an already thrilling day in the wilderness of Costa Rica.

ATV tours

Depending on the landscape and your skill level when it comes to driving, these can be a lot of fun. Investigate what you'll be riding through and read the reviews thoroughly before booking. Insurance might be a little fuzzy on this too, so make sure that won't be an additional fee.

National parks

Observing wildlife in a national park is favorable compared to a zoo. We boated down a river alongside the crocodiles who lurked in the water while monkeys played in the trees on the banks.

We've encountered certain trees that they warned us not to touch. They make the skin burn on contact, and the antidote is another tree's bark to counter the effect. Stay on the trail and obey your guide. Your never know where the wildlife is lurking!

Chapter 10
Heading Home

Last day blues

Inevitably, the vacation week must come to an end. Two or three days out, you and your partner might sense it, but the word "home" becomes taboo. It's hard not to experience at least a little anxiety about returning to the real world. Your skin, stomach and liver might be ready, but if you've had a great vacation, the last full day can be somber.

Make sure you confirm what time your shuttle is picking you up that next morning, and have the voucher handy. Many resorts offer a service where you can take care of checkout matters the night before. This involves settling up any bills for your room and filling out a survey. They'll give you a checkout card which you'll need to board the shuttle upon leaving.

Exiting the pool on the final full day is sad because I have to say goodbye to my favorite bartenders. I grow envious of the pale-skinned guests who just arrived that day and have an entire fun-filled week ahead of them. And while it's tempting to tie one on one last night, it probably isn't smart to risk a hangover on departure day.

Before your final dinner, double-check that your passports (and immigration cards) are in the safe. Begin rounding up your clothes and other loose items scattered around the room. Hang your swimsuits up so they dry before morning. Tip anyone who's been especially friendly and helpful throughout the week.

There's no shame in calling it an early night on the final evening. It can be challenging to not fret over tomorrow's travel. On the day we depart, I usually wake up early to catch the sunrise before dipping my toes in the ocean one last time. At this point all you can do is reminisce about the wonderful week and start planning ahead for the next trip.

What's the process like on the travel day?

Hurry up and wait.

You should arrange for a bellhop to transport your luggage to the lobby. Hopefully you're not required to leave before breakfast, because it's going to be a long day. You'll turn in your keycards and wait with the rest of the melancholy bunch who are scheduled to be on the same shuttle.

If your shuttle leaves before breakfast is available, order room service or hoard some fruit the day before.

All resorts feel the need to get you to the airport at least three hours before your plane leaves. They do this as a precaution in case something goes wrong, and because they need you out of your rooms so that new guests can check in. Boarding the shuttle home is depressing, and you'll notice a much different vibe compared to the ride there.

When you arrive at the airport, there will be men waiting to cart your luggage for you. If you allow them, be sure you can tip. One year we had to tip a man $10 because we were out of smaller bills. Now we make sure to grab our suitcases ourselves.

The one highlight of the return home is the duty-free liquor store at the airport. You should be able to find some great deals (although at this point in the week it sometimes feels like you'll never drink again). Research the amount of alcohol you're legally allowed to bring home (currently no more than 5 liters). When you buy it, they'll need your passport. The package is to stay sealed until after your flight, because obviously, large open bottles of liquor on a plane are illegal.

We squeeze in a last order of nachos or something lighter before taking off. Yes, there's the typical price-gouging, but a restaurant can offer a better seat than your flight's gate area where you'll inevitably sit by a family of six with no control over their hyped-up children. Or if you're not that hungry, an unopened packaged snack from home is beneficial and cheaper. I always hide one from myself so that I don't get into it during the trip.

More airports are offering free Wi-Fi, but a book and some headphones should be in your carry-on just in case.

On the flight home you have to fill out a form declaring anything you've acquired on your trip. List your purchases and the costs. You get a generous limit before you have to pay any taxes or fill out excess paperwork. It's only one form per household, and it's not complicated.

The final obstacle after your flight is U.S. Customs. This process takes a while, and you're not allowed to have your cellphone out while you wait. They'll ask you about being around livestock, about bringing food home, and then they'll question you about any other souvenirs mentioned on your form. After that, you just have to wait on your luggage. Don't be surprised if they dig through your suitcase. I like to pack all my dirty underwear on top in an act of rebellion.

What am I not allowed to bring back home?

Any sort of plants or fresh foods are not allowed. If you buy tequila, they'll ask you about limes. You cannot bring mamajuana (the official liquor of their country) back from the Dominican Republic. The bottle contains vegetation and roots, and they don't want any new species of plants imported.

When you finally get home, treat yourself to some American food, tap water, and television while you let your body transition back to normal. I highly recommend at least a week of detox before drinking again. You might experience a bit of depression as you return to the real world, because your brain hasn't been making its daily amount of dopamine thanks to the alcohol.

If you took my advice and laid off on social media until your return home, you can post your pictures and bask in the "likes" and comments for a few days. Now you're the couple that everyone is envious of!

Now it's your turn

With the amount of money my wife and I have spent on vacations, we could've put a severe dent in our mortgage. But then, once the mortgage was paid off, what would we do with the extra money? Travel, of course. That's why we figured, why not live it up while we're still mobile? These vacations, normally taken in March and July, are part of the foundation to our marriage. From the time we book our trip to the time the jet goes wheels up, we immerse ourselves in vacation talk. Half of the fun is the countdown and anticipation.

When I was a child, my family wasn't able to take any international vacations. The furthest we traveled was from Ohio to Oklahoma. The five of us piled into our family car (not even an SUV) and motored countless hours to a landlocked relative's house. I loved it at the time, but I could not imagine experiencing something as great as an all-inclusive resort. On vacation, I have the chance to act like a child again if I want. There's no judgment.

The pictures we take, the inside jokes we share, and the memories we make are irreplaceable. I can even name all eighteen trips we've taken in order. Even the trips to value resorts were wonderful. There have never been any nightmare weeks. Yes, there's the occasional bug or rainy afternoon, but we've never had what would be considered a terrible day (other than the days spent returning home).

Start saving and begin researching the best resort for you and your loved ones—then begin your countdown to paradise!

Appendix A

Resorts we've stayed at...

May 2009, March 2014—Grand Bávaro Princess in Punta Cana, Dominican Republic

May 2010—Marival in Puerto Vallarta, Mexico

May 2011—Riu Resort in Guanacaste, Costa Rica

May 2012—Now Jade in Riviera Cancun, Mexico

March 2013—Riu Palace in Guanacaste, Costa Rica

July 2013, 2014, 2015, 2017, 2018—Secrets Capri in Riviera Cancun, Mexico

March 2015—Hotel Riu Emerald Bay in Mazatlán, Mexico

July 2016—Secrets Silversands in Riviera Cancun, Mexico

March 2016, 2017, 2018, 2019—Secrets Resort in Hualtuco, Mexico

July 2019—Valentin Imperial Maya in Riviera Cancun, Mexico

Appendix B

What to do when...

3 to 6 months out

*Research and decide on which resort you want
*Begin checking prices on website daily
*Be sure passports are valid, if not, order ASAP
*Schedule vacation days off from work
*Book trip and pay for at least half of it
*Begin workout regimen and diet for beach body (optional)

1 month out

*Make final payment on balance of trip
*Research and book a day trip
*Shop for any necessary clothing or footwear

1 to 2 weeks out

*Schedule mail to be placed on hold via USPS.com
*Make arrangements for house sitters/pet sitters
*Finalize list of things to pack
*Arrange travel to and from your airport and confirm what time you need to arrive
*Purchase snacks for travel days
*Withdraw tipping money (stack of ones and fives) and all other necessary cash from bank
*Begin packing
*Stock up on all hygienic and medicinal needs
*Inform trusted neighbor of your trip
*Stock up on reading material
*Expose skin to moderate sunlight if possible

1 day out

*Have passports out on counter
*Prepare list for departure morning
*Clear wallet/purse of unnecessary items
*Inform bank and credit card companies that you're traveling
*Double-check packing list with suitcase
*Prepare carry-on bag
*Confirm flight time and ride to airport
*Change outgoing voicemail message
*Set up email away message
*Set out clothes you're wearing for travel
*Get to bed early and set multiple alarms

Morning of departure

*Take out any garbage to trash can
*Adjust thermostat
*Unplug any small appliances
*Set security system and lighting
*Pack phone chargers
*Turn off waterline
*Have passports in hand

Appendix C

Additional Resources:

Get more trip advice and reviews from my YouTube Channel: Robagain2.

Travelocity.com has the most reviews on resorts and day trips.

 Rob Durham is a high school language arts teacher and stand-up comedian. When he's not in the classroom or touring stages around the Midwest, you can find him planted at the swim-up bar. Rob and his lovely wife, Beth continue to travel and post about their adventures to their favorite resorts.

Follow
www.RobDurhamComedy.com

Additional Titles

Don't Wear Shorts on Stage: The Stand-up Guide to Comedy

Around the Block

Made in the USA
Monee, IL
02 February 2023

25952613R00066